Current
CONTROVERSIES

Privacy and Security
in the Digital Age

Other Books in the Current Controversies Series

Privacy and Security in the Digital Age

Anne Cunningham, Book Editor

GREENHAVEN
PUBLISHING

Published in 2017 by Greenhaven Publishing, LLC
353 3rd Avenue, Suite 255, New York, NY 10010

Copyright © 2017 by Greenhaven Publishing, LLC

First Edition

Articles in Greenhaven Publishing anthologies are often edited for length to meet page
requirements. In addition, original titles of these works are changed to clearly present
the main thesis and to explicitly indicate the author's opinion. Every effort is made to
ensure that Greenhaven Publishing accurately reflects the original intent of the authors.
Every effort has been made to trace the owners of the copyrighted material.

Cover image: ymgerman / Shutterstock.com

Library of Congress Cataloging-in-Publication Data

Names: Cunningham, Anne.
Title: Privacy and security in the digital age / Anne Cunningham.
Description: New York : Greenhaven Publishing, 2017. |
Series: Current controversies | Includes index.
Identifiers: LCCN ISBN 9781534500327 (pbk.) | ISBN 9781534500211 (library bound)
Subjects: LCSH: Privacy, Right of—United States—Juvenile literature. | Internet—
Security measures—United States—Juvenile literature. | Data protection—United
States—Juvenile literature. | Computer security—United States—Juvenile literature.
Classification: LCC JC599.U5 C75 2017 | DDC 323.44'802854678—dc23

Manufactured in the United States of America

Website: http://greenhavenpublishing.com

Contents

Chapter 1: Is Security More Important Than Liberty?

Charles Stimson and Andrew Grossman
Ideally, there is no tradeoff between security and freedom—
these should be mutually reinforcing values. The framers of the
Constitution designed the US political system with checks and
balances to prevent any branch of government from becoming too
powerful. There is every reason to be optimistic that this structure
will enable the country to withstand future threats to liberty
and security.

Ron Iphofen
In the digital age, privacy may already be an antiquated concern.
Facebook, Google, and other companies know quite a bit about
us already. But this is not necessarily a cause for alarm. Rather, we
should harness this technology for the greater good and to prevent
atrocities and harm.

Tim Mayfield
In Australia, the threat of "lone wolf" terror attacks may be serious
enough to justify minor infringements on personal liberty. Although
unscrupulous politicians use fear to advance an agenda, the privacy
tradeoff for increased national security may nonetheless be necessary.

Chapter 2: Does the Government Have the Right to Monitor Its Citizens?

Chapter 4: Does Video Surveillance Make Us Safer?

author poses the question "how much surveillance should democracy have?" and recommends far less than our current level.

Surveillance Inhibits Moral Decision Making

Emrys Westacott

Even if surveillance efforts did increase safety, what is the moral impact? If the presence of cameras hampers criminal acts, it does so for the wrong reasons. Declining to commit a crime because you'll get caught is not the same thing as declining to commit a crime because it's the wrong thing to do. Surveillance will hinder our moral development.

Surveillance Cameras Are a Slippery Slope

American Civil Liberties Union of Illinois

As the technology of video surveillance systems becomes more sophisticated, concerns arise. Given the history of unlawful political surveillance in cities like Chicago, measures must be taken to protect the rights of those being recorded.

Foreword

"Controversy" is a word that has an undeniably unpleasant connotation. It carries a definite negative charge. Controversy can spoil family gatherings, spread a chill around classroom and campus discussion, inflame public discourse, open raw civic wounds, and lead to the ouster of public officials. We often feel that controversy is almost akin to bad manners, a rude and shocking eruption of that which must not be spoken or thought of in polite, tightly guarded society. To avoid controversy, to quell controversy, is often seen as a public good, a victory for etiquette, perhaps even a moral or ethical imperative.

Yet the studious, deliberate avoidance of controversy is also a whitewashing, a denial, a death threat to democracy. It is a false sterilizing and sanitizing and superficial ordering of the messy, ragged, chaotic, at times ugly processes by which a healthy democracy identifies and confronts challenges, engages in passionate debate about appropriate approaches and solutions, and arrives at something like a consensus and a broadly accepted and supported way forward. Controversy is the megaphone, the speaker's corner, the public square through which the citizenry finds and uses its voice. Controversy is the life's blood of our democracy and absolutely essential to the vibrant health of our society.

Our present age is certainly no stranger to controversy. We are consumed by fierce debates about technology, privacy, political correctness, poverty, violence, crime and policing, guns, immigration, civil and human rights, terrorism, militarism, environmental protection, and gender and racial equality. Loudly competing voices are raised every day, shouting opposing opinions, putting forth competing agendas, and summoning starkly different visions of a utopian or dystopian future. Often these voices attempt to shout the others down; there is precious little listening and considering among the cacophonous din. Yet listening and considering, too, are essential to the health of a democracy. If controversy is democracy's lusty lifeblood, respectful listening and careful thought are its higher faculties, its brain, its conscience.

Current Controversies does not shy away from or attempt to hush the loudly competing voices. It seeks to provide readers with as wide and representative as possible a range of articulate voices on any given controversy of the day, separates each one out to allow it to be heard clearly and fairly, and encourages careful listening to each of these well-crafted, thoughtfully expressed opinions, supplied by some of today's leading academics, thinkers, analysts, politicians, policy makers, economists, activists, change agents, and advocates. Only after listening to a wide range of opinions on an issue, evaluating the strengths and weaknesses of each argument, assessing how well the facts and available evidence mesh with the stated opinions and conclusions, and thoughtfully and critically examining one's own beliefs and conscience can the reader begin to arrive at his or her own conclusions and articulate his or her own stance on the spotlighted controversy.

This process is facilitated and supported in each Current Controversies volume by an introduction and chapter overviews that provide readers with the essential context they need to begin engaging with the spotlighted controversies, with the debates surrounding them, and with their own perhaps shifting or nascent opinions on them. Chapters are organized around several key questions that are answered with diverse opinions representing all points on the political spectrum. In its content, organization, and methodology, readers are encouraged to determine the authors' point of view and purpose, interrogate and analyze the various arguments and their rhetoric and structure, evaluate the arguments' strengths and weaknesses, test their claims against available facts and evidence, judge the validity of the reasoning, and bring into clearer, sharper focus the reader's own beliefs and conclusions and how they may differ from or align with those in the collection or those of classmates.

Research has shown that reading comprehension skills improve dramatically when students are provided with compelling, intriguing, and relevant "discussable" texts. The subject matter of these collections could not be more compelling, intriguing, or urgently relevant to today's students and the world they are poised to inherit. The anthologized articles also provide the basis for stimulating, lively, and passionate classroom debates. Students who are compelled to anticipate objections to their own argument and identify the flaws in those of an opponent read more carefully, think more critically, and steep themselves in relevant context, facts, and information more thoroughly. In short, using discussable text of the kind provided by every single volume in the Current Controversies series encourages close reading, facilitates reading comprehension, fosters research, strengthens critical thinking, and greatly enlivens and energizes classroom discussion and participation. The entire learning process is deepened, extended, and strengthened.

If we are to foster a knowledgeable, responsible, active, and engaged citizenry, we must provide readers with the intellectual, interpretive, and critical-thinking tools and experience necessary to make sense of the world around them and of the all-important debates and arguments that inform it. We must encourage them not to run away from or attempt to quell controversy but to embrace it in a responsible, conscientious, and thoughtful way, to sharpen and strengthen their own informed opinions by listening to and critically analyzing those of others. This series encourages respectful engagement with and analysis of current controversies and competing opinions and fosters a resulting increase in the strength and rigor of one's own opinions and stances. As such, it helps readers assume their rightful place in the public square and provides them with the skills necessary to uphold their awesome responsibility—guaranteeing the continued and future health of a vital, vibrant, and free democracy.

Introduction

> "I'm often asked the question, 'What's
> more important—civil liberties
> or national security?' It's a false
> question; it's a false choice. At the
> end of the day, we must do both, and
> they are not irreconcilable."
>
> –John C. Inglis, NSA deputy
> director, January 2009

The year 2013 was a watershed year for the issue of privacy. Until then, most Americans assumed their privacy was a basic right protected by the Fourth Amendment of the constitution, and enshrined in our political culture and societal values. Many citizens were certainly aware of so-called "big data"—the sophisticated information mining and algorithms used by Silicon Valley firms to track our proclivities and preferences, primarily for online commerce and marketing. Yet aside from a few observers, most of us accepted this technology as benign, or at worst, mildly annoying.

This state of affairs changed irrevocably in 2013 with the Global Surveillance Disclosures, a shocking cache of authenticated documents leaked by former National Security Agency (NSA) contractor Edward Snowden. These documents exposed a secret global surveillance network operated by a consortium of governmental intelligence agencies from Great Britain, Australia, Canada, Germany, and the United States, among others. These documents revealed a massive surveillance program operated with the tacit consent, if not explicit participation, of private technology and telecommunications firms. In fact, some companies even received direct cash payments from the NSA for allowing access to private data. Suddenly, the harvesting of online and cellular information appeared far less innocuous. Snowden was promptly charged with espionage and found political asylum in Russia, where he remains to this day.

The political fallout from these revelations was enormous. President Obama quickly attempted to justify the US surveillance efforts, explaining that the government had no interest in spying on ordinary Americans, but rather was seeking patterns of "metadata" that could prove crucial in matters of counterterrorism and national security. Obama claimed Snowden's actions brought "more heat than light" and defended the NSA's controversial practices. Nonetheless, in May of 2015, a federal appeals court ruled that the NSA's collection of bulk data was illegal and ordered the program shut down.

Once exposed, government and law enforcement predictably invoked national security, "law and order," and safety to justify their arguably intrusive harvesting of private information. Indeed, national security has since become the perennial flipside to privacy. While the two values are now generally understood to be in tension, this has not always been the case in our nation's history. The current paradigm of "privacy versus security" began in earnest shortly after another pivotal moment in US history: the 9/11 attacks.

On October 26, 2001, George W. Bush signed the Patriot Act into law. (Its full title is Uniting and Strengthening America by Providing Appropriate Tools Required to Intercept and Obstruct Terrorism Act of 2001.) This law provided federal and local law enforcement with broad latitude to circumvent existing laws restricting surveillance. The Patriot Act also enabled the collection of bulk data, the monitoring of foreign nationals, wiretapping, and other intelligence gathering tools. Proponents praised this measure as the proper recalibration of security versus liberty in a new, more dangerous world order. Defenders of civil liberties argued that the act violated the Bill of Rights. According to polling, the majority of American citizens were comfortable with the Patriot Act, despite the concessions to privacy it entailed. Thus began the descent into the surveillance culture eventually exposed by Snowden.

Of course, in an age when periodic terror attacks are a reality, safety and security cannot be taken lightly, even if this requires some concessions to privacy. Such would be the clear-cut conclusion, if the success rates of data collection and video surveillance were not so decidedly mixed. For example, in notable cases such as the Boston Marathon bombing, video surveillance was instrumental in identifying the perpetrators. However, in the vast majority of counterterrorism cases, traditional means of intelligence such as community policing and embedded agents have yielded far better results. Only an estimated 3 percent of antiterrorist tips were aided by NSA bulk surveillance. In the United Kingdom, surveillance cameras are ubiquitous. Nonetheless, peer-reviewed studies have concluded that the effect of widespread surveillance on crime rates is statistically insignificant.

If increased surveillance violates privacy and does not yield particularly impressive results, why is it such a priority to continue? Some have suggested that in a society marked by radically unequal wealth distribution, powerful surveillance is a way to ensure that mass movements do not gain significant traction. For elites, this is a cheaper way to retain power than the granting of material concessions to placate a potentially violent oppressed population. Even if we dismiss such suspicions as conspiratorial, the collection of data is nonetheless highly profitable in the private and public sector alike. Finally, there is the technological capability and the abstract pursuit of "pure" information to contend with. If we have the capability to learn so much about ourselves, why should a potentially antiquated notion like privacy stand in the way?

These are the questions to consider as you examine the viewpoints contained herein. As many have stated, just because you have nothing to hide does not mean that the implications of diminished privacy are not serious—and even dangerous.

Is Security More Important Than Liberty?

Overview: National Security and Civil Liberties in America

Charles Stimson and Andrew Grossman

Charles D. Stimson is senior legal fellow and Andrew M. Grossman is senior legal policy analyst in the Center for Legal and Judicial Studies at The Heritage Foundation.

The United States was born into war with the Declaration of Independence, the most important statement of liberty and natural rights ever made. Since then, America has been the world's freest country and has become its most secure, with a military equal to any threat. America has avoided the fate of nations that have traded freedoms for promises of security, or security for unlimited freedom, and achieved neither. Yet the healthy fear that one or the other will disappear has been present in every era since the Founding. How must America balance security and civil liberties?

"Among the many objects to which a wise and free people find it necessary to direct their attention, that of providing for their safety seems to be first."[1] So wrote John Jay in *The Federalist*, in which the Constitution's leading Framers explained the government on which they hoped to build America.

The founding generation knew firsthand the oppression of tyranny. The litany of British abuses and usurpations is cited in the Declaration of Independence: lawless decrees, the quartering of troops, wholesale plunder, and deprivation of liberty and life according to whim, not law. To the Founders, these were violations of both man's natural rights and of the security that a sovereign is obliged to provide the people. In such circumstances, "it is their right, it is their duty, to throw off such Government, and to provide new Guards for their future security."

"How Must America Balance Security and Liberty," Charles Stimson and Andrew Grossman, The Heritage Foundation, December 9, 2011. Reprinted by permission.

And so they did, and the nation was thrust into war. From the first, Americans saw liberty and security as one and the same, and not in opposition.

Although we often speak of the proper "balance" between security and liberty, the two need not be in tension. Policies that make the nation more secure, particularly against foreign threats, do not necessarily undermine its people's liberty. Protecting individual liberty does not invariably hobble the nation's defense. Rather, as the Constitution recognizes, the two are reinforcing: we "secure the Blessings of Liberty to ourselves and our Posterity." A threat to America's security is also a threat to Americans' liberties.

"In framing a government which is to be administered by men over men," observed James Madison, "the great difficulty lies in this: you must first enable the government to control the governed; and in the next place oblige it to control itself."[2] Almost all nations achieve control of the governed, though more often by force than by consent. Limits on the power of governments are rarer, and more complex. Yet they are essential to preserving both security and liberty. This problem was the Framers' chief concern in drafting the Constitution, and their solution was radical and brilliant.

The problem they faced was the one identified deftly by Ronald Reagan: "The kind of government that is strong enough to give you everything you need is also strong enough to take away everything that you have." Any power delegated by the people to their government may be abused and used against them. History is replete with examples of such oppression, and it remains common today.

But it has not happened in America. The Constitution's Framers placed their faith not in specific guarantees of rights—those came later—but in an elegant system of checks on government. Foremost is the separation of power between the three branches of the federal government, as well as between the federal government and the states. These arrangements provide the flexibility necessary to ensure security and the restraint essential to safeguard liberties.

A dramatic example came with President Truman's attempt to seize private property to further the Korean War effort. Claiming his actions were justified by national security, Truman authorized the Commerce Secretary to take control of the nation's steel industry. Within weeks, the matter was before the Supreme Court, which rebuffed Truman's claim that he had the power to act without, and even contrary to, any law enacted by Congress.

Justice Jackson's famous concurrence hit on the danger of the President's position: "Presidential claim to a power at once so conclusive and preclusive must be scrutinized with caution, for what is at stake is the equilibrium established by our constitutional system."[3] By contrast, "When the President acts pursuant to an express or implied authorization of Congress, his authority is at its maximum." When the political branches are in agreement, Jackson recognized, security and liberty are most likely to go hand in hand.

The government is also checked by the ballot. When the branches of the federal government have conspired to abrogate the people's liberties, the people have responded. In 1798, President John Adams and his Federalist allies in Congress passed the Sedition Act, which criminalized "false, scandalous and malicious" speech concerning the government, Congress, or the President. The Act was intended to suppress criticism of naval warfare with France, and it was a clear violation of Americans' rights to speak freely and to question their government's actions.

Instead of suppressing dissent, the Act ignited a political firestorm, as states passed resolutions denouncing the law and candidates ran on their opposition to it. The Federalists, including Adams, were swept out of office, and President Thomas Jefferson, who succeeded Adams, pardoned those serving sentences under the Act.

The protections codified in the Bill of Rights are the final firewall against any intrusions on liberty that would unravel the checks in the Constitution. For example, without the First Amendment's guarantee of the right to free speech, to assemble, and to petition government, the political branches would be less responsive to citizens' concerns, and voters would be less informed of the significance of their choices. The Fourth Amendment's prohibition on unreasonable searches and seizures ensures that the government may not arbitrarily harass those who oppose its policies. The Fifth Amendment's Takings Clause requires the burden of government policies to be shared broadly.

While they are important, these enumerated rights are also narrow and specific. They are only an infinitesimal portion of the rights retained by the states and the people. For example, you have the right to provide for your family, to direct the upbringing of your children, to make contracts, and to own a house. These rights, which are too numerous to list and too changing to set forth in a constitution, are subject not to specific guarantees but to the Constitution's structural protections. Thus, most matters of national security and liberty are fit not for adjudication by the courts, but for the exercise of the judgment of the people through the political branches.

By and large, the United States has succeeded in preserving security and civil liberties by adopting policies that reinforce both. When it has departed from that course, both liberty and security have suffered.

Military strength under firm civilian control is the best guarantor of liberty. Thomas Jefferson observed "Whatever enables us to go to war, secures our peace."[4] So it was in the Cold War, when U.S. strength and the system of government that underpinned it led to an American victory without a great war, and brought the greatest expansion in liberty in the history of the world.

By contrast, America's Cold War enemies sought to achieve military supremacy by planning and central control, organizing their people and their economies around the needs of the state, and denying their citizens' most basic freedoms. But their ostentatious displays of strength—parades, flyovers, fleets—were hollow. They were the products of governments that were at war with the security and liberties of their peoples.

The United States today faces the opposite risk. Maintaining a strong national defense secures liberty against threats known and unknown, from rogue states to terrorist organizations. This is the paramount and vital responsibility of the federal government.

Intelligence-gathering, when effectively performed in ways consistent with Americans' rights and expectations, is similarly essential. Such intelligence programs help to secure our liberties against those who seek to destroy them. The better these programs work, the more they protect our security and liberty.

A perfect example is the use of military tribunals for terrorists. The use of tribunals in the United States dates back to the Revolutionary War, and has always been viewed as providing necessary flexibility in military operations, especially compared to the customary alternative, summary execution. Today, tribunals serve an additional function as a wall between our civilian justice system and the lawful compromises that must be made in trying violations of the laws of war.

At times, the United States has made decisions that were counterproductive. While imprisoning those who actively conspire with the enemy in a time of war is sound policy, the internment of Japanese citizens because of their ethnicity during World War II was both unconstitutional and highly destructive of liberty. It was also counterproductive, diverting resources and attention, costing valuable manpower, and directly harming the war effort. The Sedition Act of 1798 was an abomination that, if anything, harmed America's political system and made the nation less safe. But America has learned well from these mistakes, and is unlikely to repeat them.

In Benjamin Franklin's memorable saying, "They that can give up essential liberty to purchase a little temporary safety deserve neither liberty nor safety." To this could be added that those willing to sacrifice liberty for security will, in the end, achieve neither. The proper way to balance security and liberty is not to balance them at all; it is to insist on policies that maximize both to the extent practicable.

Endnotes

1. John Jay, "Concerning Dangers From Foreign Force and Influence (cont'd)," *Federalist* No. 3, at *http://www.foundingfathers.info/federalistpapers/fed03.htm*
2. James Madison, "The Structure of the Government Must Furnish the Proper Checks and Balances Between the Different Departments," *Federalist* No. 51, at *http://www.foundingfathers.info/federalistpapers/fed51.htm*
3. *Youngstown Sheet & Tube Co. v. Sawyer.* 343 U.S. 579 U.S. Supreme Court, 1952.
4. Thomas Jefferson, letter to James Monroe, October 24, 1823.

Let's Not Worry About Privacy, Security is More Important

Ron Iphofen

Ron Iphofen is an independent research consultant. He was formerly director of postgraduate studies, health sciences, Bangor University.

I n 2013, I submitted a commentary piece to *Times Higher Education* that concluded as follows: "I am now of the opinion that privacy has to be sacrificed for the sake of security. What matters most in times of crisis? That people won't be able to find out who we are, where we are and when? Or that by accurate surveillance, by technologically sophisticated watchfulness and by cautious tracking of anyone exhibiting suspicious behavior, disaster can be averted, lives saved and misery avoided? It is a matter of finding the lesser evil. When the next multiple killing occurs, will the loved ones of those murdered be placated by the rationale that nothing could be done to prevent it since people's right to privacy had to be protected?"

Those words never made it into the final article, which focused on the extent to which universities could and should monitor staff emails ("Do they see all @ac.uk?," Opinion, September 5, 2013). But I am more convinced than ever that they should be heard given the recent instances of such multiple murders in Paris, California, Brussels and Lahore. I strongly suspect that, given the available technology, much more could have been done to anticipate and possibly even prevent those atrocities had it not been for the privacy-related "obstacles" placed in the way.

It is not that I don't value privacy; it is rather that I do not expect that large aspects of my life can ever be considered private

---

"Safety Is More Important Than Privacy," Ron Iphofen, *Times Higher Education*, April 28, 2016. Reprinted by permission.

again. If privacy is not exactly "dead", it is certainly staggering about uncertainly.

There have been a range of revelations over recent years vindicating the view that privacy cannot be ensured in the modern, technological age. These include the newspaper phone-hacking scandal; a bug in Facebook's data archive exposing the personal details of about 6 million people; the "mistaken" collection of data by Google's Street View equipment in 30 countries (including complete email messages, logging-in details and medical listings); and, of course, Edward Snowden's whistleblowing of the automated interrogation of international communications by US and UK intelligence agencies. Some commentators, such as Kelvin Wade, have even announced that privacy is "a 20th-century concept." And surveillance from all sources has grown rapidly in line with technological developments and the assumed rise in threats to public safety.

My own heightened awareness of the issue comes from acting as an ethics adviser in a European public transport security project, known as SECUR-ED. Surveillance has become routine in most public transport settings but privacy, human rights and data protection laws all mediate the relationship between the transport "authority" and the passenger. Personal data cannot be collected indiscriminately. It can be collected only to address a specific and identifiable problem and, even then, prior checks under local and national data protection regulations apply.

SECUR-ED alone was funded to the tune of more than €40 million (£32 million), and there are nearly 200 other security-related European Union projects. These involve academics from across the Continent and the disciplines, including ethicists, engineers, communications technologists, biomedical scientists and systems designers. But although ethicists and surveillance technologists can and do work hand in hand on many of these projects, the fundamental contradiction between privacy and security ensures that this remains an uneasy alliance. It is one that some human rights activists resist joining, preferring to remain in their "camp" to fight for privacy untainted by compromise. And no doubt some surveillers are content for them to do so and refrain from interfering in their work. One can only assume that both are high-mindedly seeking a free and safe society. It is just that they profoundly differ in the fundamental principles upon which they think such a society can be founded.

We typically take for granted our ability to walk down a familiar street at any time of day or night and not feel at risk of harm from others. Our complacency is challenged only when we learn that an unarmed soldier out of uniform can, for example, be hacked to death in broad daylight on the streets of London. Or that many innocent bystanders enjoying the finish to a marathon in Boston can be blown to pieces (with the whole event recorded on mobile phones). Yes, privacy is precious, but so too is our security. And when we ask the authorities to help us to attain both, we confront them with a dilemma. I want them to respect my privacy, but perhaps not the privacy of those planning to do harm to me or my community. I want them to keep me secure by securing those who threaten my security.

A 2013 editorial in *The Guardian* on the undercover investigation by the Metropolitan Police's Special Demonstration Squad (SDS) into murdered black teenager Stephen Lawrence's family complained: "This is the kind of thing that happens when, without adequate legal restraint, fears for security are allowed to take priority over privacy." What needs establishing is when such "fears for security" (talk of which implicitly suggests overreaction) are unjustified; in other words, when and how the "adequate legal restraint" can be applied, and by whom. There is rarely a situation in which security can be protected without the expense of some loss of privacy.

It is obviously true that privacy was more easily protected in the past. But starting with the ability to steam open glued envelopes, through photographic reproduction and phone tapping to automated hacking devices and GPS tracking, as the technology of data handling has grown in sophistication, so too has the means to "interrogate" it. Now human rights advocates seek "privacy by design" for communications technology. But if techniques such as encryption exist, so too do the means to circumvent them. In the wake of the Edward Snowden affair, Apple made great play of its refusal to help the FBI hack into one of the San Bernardino shooters' iPhones, claiming that to do so would potentially compromise the privacy of all its customers. But, in the end, the FBI reportedly gained access to the phone with the help of "professional hackers." That point also highlights the fact that the means to invade privacy are not the exclusive preserve of well-intentioned state authorities. Human rights watchers refer routinely to the chilling effects of knowing that the state can invade our privacy in so many ways. Personally, I find it even more chilling that those whom I trust much less than the state may be doing that too.

One thing is certain: even if we restrict or ban "good" people from carrying out covert surveillance, there are plenty of "bad" people who will ignore such restrictions and carry on employing the technology for their own nefarious interests regardless. Quite simply, the technology is there and available for anyone to use. I have witnessed the use of behavioural tracking devices, facial recognition software and "sniffing" technologies that can detect explosive substances.

There are several types of technology that could have flagged up the Brussels airport suicide bombers for wearing gloves on only one hand, potentially allowing them to be intercepted before they detonated their devices. Indeed, if a generic surveillance technology of the sort that Snowden blew the lid on had been in operation, their intent might have been disclosed even before they donned their suicide belts. It is also worth remembering that investigative journalists and social science researchers (ethnographers or anthropologists usually) also use their own form of covert surveillance, subject to the limits imposed by the law and ethics committees, as well as social mores and their own consciences. Judgements about applicants' real purpose and intent remain a standard problem for formal research ethics review—they can limit the work of the well-intentioned, while those less well-intentioned will deceive and dissemble to continue their activities regardless of the moral judgements of others.

The problem lies in the extrapolation of concern. Just because some people or agencies have abused their position does not mean that all surveillance is unfair, unjust or badly conceived. The undercover monitoring of the Lawrence family or the use of the identities of dead babies by undercover SDS agents merely illustrates how not to conduct such work. Whatever the concerns might have been at the time about race-related riots or criminal activity, it is clear that such approaches were not authorised at a higher governmental level—and the political checks and balances of a democratic society should generally limit the risks of such abuse.

It is noteworthy in this regard that there are many local variations about where people think the balance should lie regarding privacy and security. Views in Germany and France are much stronger than, say, in the UK about the right to privacy—as demonstrated by the fuss in the former over the use of graffiti-spotting drones by railway company Deutsche Bahn. Indeed, on an even more topical note, sensitivities in Panama about privacy must be particularly acute if the co-founder of the Mossack Fonseca law firm is at all representative of his countrymen. Responding to the leak of thousands of the firm's documents, highlighting the huge extent of tax avoidance by the global elite, Ramon Fonseca complained that "there is an internaftional campaign against privacy [which] is a sacred human right." Then again, it is perhaps not surprising that a man in his line of work would hold to such a principle.

Ethics has always been about weighing harms and benefits. Regarding Snowden's whistleblowing, for instance, the key questions would be whether the benefits of his actions (alerting the general public to breaches of their privacy) outweigh the harms (letting terrorists know that they are being watched). The judicious outcome is achieved when most people perceive the inevitable compromise, balancing the harms and benefits, to be tolerable.

There is one final point to make about the growth of sophisticated surveillance technology, whether covert or overt. That is that it appears to have almost entirely supplanted the old-fashioned undercover operative. Those fixated by the past excesses of the SDS may well be comforted by that, but it is one reason that terrorism is flourishing. The terrorists responsible for the Paris and Brussels atrocities were an intimate network that didn't even need to communicate via hackable mobile phones: they lived in each other's communities and houses. Only an embedded agent could have monitored them effectively. The ethics of such intimate infiltration remain complex to negotiate, but it is senseless and potentially suicidal to take the view that it is never justified.

There is no denying that effective counterterrorism can require enhanced state oppression, but terrorism is itself a form of oppression—and a much less democratic form. I, for one, am entirely happy to sacrifice some of my privacy rights to ensure my security and that of my loved ones.

Enhanced Counter-terrorism Measures are Reasonable

Tim Mayfield

Tim Mayfield is the executive officer to the chancellor of Australian National University and previously worked for Australia's Department of Foreign Affairs and Trade and Department of Defense.

In his cautionary piece regarding the Government's proposed metadata retention policy, Mathew Beard correctly points out that: "liberty and security exist on a sliding scale: the more liberty one possesses, the more one exposes oneself to risk of attack."

I agree with him on this point. However, I would argue that the proposed enhancements to Australia's counter-terrorism framework are one instance where it may be both justified and necessary to shift this balance toward ensuring our collective security.

The recent proposal by the Government to toughen Australia's anti-terror laws has led to serious concerns being expressed by some commentators regarding their potential impact on the basic rule of law and our collective rights and freedoms. While these concerns are valid, they need to be balanced with an acknowledgement that such rights do not exist in isolation of the equally fundamental responsibility of government to ensure the safety and security of its citizens.

ASIO Director-General David Irvine and AFP Deputy Commissioner Andrew Colvin today held a press conference to clarify what the compulsory two-year retention of metadata by telcos meant and how it would be used by law enforcement agencies.

In an effort to quell concern, Irvine stressed the plan wasn't about mass surveillance nor mass invasion of privacy, and agencies would still require a warrant to access certain information.

"Maybe We Should Give Up A Bit Of Liberty," Tim Mayfield, Abc.net, August 8, 2014. Reprinted by permission.

Certainly, enhancement to government power in any sphere, but especially in matters of criminal justice, should be met with caution and only implemented after extensive consultation and careful drafting of the laws in question.

Unfortunately, that does not appear to have been the case with the Government's rushed announcement of data retention by telecommunications companies. Likewise, the real test of the beefed up terrorism offences will come with the introduction to Parliament of the Counter-Terrorism Foreign Fighters Bill later this year.

Nevertheless, this does not mean that the measures are without merit.

While it is incumbent upon the media and our politicians not to fan the flames of fear or to use the spectre of terrorism for political ends, they also have a responsibility to soberly and methodically assess such threats as they emerge and put in place reasonable and proportionate measures in response.

Indeed, those that accuse the Government of manufacturing the security threat to distract from other matters should note that of the 30 Australians that were known to be fighting against Western forces in Afghanistan, 25 came back home and two-thirds of those that returned to Australia were subsequently involved in planning terrorist attacks.

As Julie Bishop said: "Five times that number are now of interest to our intelligence and security agencies, either already fighting overseas or planning to become involved. So this is a far greater challenge for us in sheer numbers."

Despite this, the $630 million price tag to bolster our counter-terrorism efforts is a steep one at a time of alleged budget austerity and it is right for the public to question whether it is all worth it for 150-odd misguided (albeit highly dangerous) young men fighting in Syria and Iraq.

The answer is that even small-scale "lone wolf" terrorist attacks can instill a degree of fear among the broader population that justifies, even demands, a decisive response. This is because such attacks have far-reaching consequences that go beyond the numbers of killed and maimed and lives ruined.

As Western governments have discovered in recent decades, their citizens have absolutely no tolerance for failure when it comes to combating terrorism. Any successful attack is met with detailed analysis of the clues that, if identified, may have thwarted the operation.

Experts and commentators inevitably lament the fact that, if only the government and its constituent counter-terrorism agencies had been more alert/empowered/resourced, the tragedy could have been avoided.

It is this inevitable reaction in the face of tragedy that demands the kind of measures currently proposed by the Government.

However, we also have a collective responsibility to ensure that the measures enacted in our name and in the interests of our safety and security are balanced with the freedoms and liberties that characterise our secular and democratic society.

This is the debate that is now unfolding. There are as yet many unanswered questions surrounding some of the more controversial measures put forward by the Government, especially regarding the proposal to reverse the burden of proof in instances where an individual has travelled to a designated area of conflict.

It may be that once the legislation is tabled, this particular reform represents a move too far in favour of the national security imperative. However, we should be willing to keep an open mind on this and the other measures currently under consideration.

The reality is that it is devilishly hard to gain information on the activities of Australians fighting in locations such as Afghanistan, Syria and Iraq. This fact, coupled with the intractable state of these conflicts and the disturbing images of fighters such as Mohamed Elomar and Khaled Sharrouf brandishing severed heads, should leave us in no doubt as to the seriousness of the situation.

We therefore have to ask ourselves: are we willing to accept the consequences of inaction in the face of the emerging threat posed by Australian fighters in places such as Syria and Iraq? If the answer is "no" then we need to think seriously about what sacrifices we are willing to make to avoid this eventuality.

Our Constitutional Rights Are Disappearing

Peter Van Buren

Peter Van Buren blew the whistle on US State Department waste and mismanagement during the Iraqi reconstruction in We Meant Well: How I Helped Lose the Battle for the Hearts and Minds of the Iraqi People.

H ere's a bit of history from another America: the Bill of Rights was designed to protect the people from their government. If the First Amendment's right to speak out publicly was the people's wall of security, then the Fourth Amendment's right to privacy was its buttress. It was once thought that the government should neither be able to stop citizens from speaking nor peer into their lives. Think of that as the essence of the Constitutional era that ended when those towers came down on September 11, 2001. Consider how privacy worked before 9/11 and how it works now in Post-Constitutional America.

The Fourth Amendment

A response to British King George's excessive invasions of privacy in colonial America, the Fourth Amendment pulls no punches: "The right of the people to be secure in their persons, houses, papers, and effects, against unreasonable searches and seizures, shall not be violated, and no Warrants shall issue, but upon probable cause, supported by Oath or affirmation, and particularly describing the place to be searched, and the persons or things to be seized."

In Post-Constitutional America, the government might as well have taken scissors to the original copy of the Constitution stored in the National Archives, then crumpled up the Fourth Amendment and tossed it in the garbage can. The NSA revelations of Edward

"4 Ways Your Constitutional Right to Privacy Has Been Gutted Since 9/11," Peter Van Buren / TomDispatch, June 26, 2014. Reprinted by permission.

Snowden are, in that sense, not just a shock to the conscience but to the Fourth Amendment itself: our government spies on us. All of us. Without suspicion. Without warrants. Without probable cause. Without restraint. This would qualify as "unreasonable" in our old constitutional world, but no more.

Here, then, are four ways that, in the name of American "security" and according to our government, the Fourth Amendment no longer really applies to our lives.

The Constitutional Borderline

Begin at America's borders. Most people believe they are "in" the United States as soon as they step off an international flight and are thus fully covered by the Bill of Rights. The truth has, in the twenty-first century, become infinitely more complicated as long-standing practices are manipulated to serve the expanding desires of the national security state. The mining of words and concepts for new, darker meanings is a hallmark of how things work in Post-Constitutional America.

Over the years, recognizing that certain situations could render Fourth Amendment requirements impractical or against the public interest, the Supreme Court crafted various exceptions to them. One was the "border search." The idea was that the United States should be able to protect itself by stopping and examining people entering the country. As a result, routine border searches without warrants are constitutionally "reasonable" simply by virtue of where they take place. It's a concept with a long history, enumerated by the First Congress in 1789.

Here's the twist in the present era: the definition of "border" has been changed. Upon arriving in the United States from abroad, you are not legally present in the country until allowed to enter by Department of Homeland Security (DHS) officials. You know, the guys who look into your luggage and stamp your passport. Until that moment, you exist in a legal void where the protections of the Bill of Rights and the laws of the United States do not apply. This concept also predates Post-Constitutional America and the DHS.

Remember the sorting process at Ellis Island in the late nineteenth and early twentieth centuries? No lawyers allowed there.

Those modest exceptions were all part of constitutional America. Today, once reasonable searches at the border have morphed into a vast "Constitution-free zone." The "border" is now a strip of land circling the country and extending 100 miles inland that includes two-thirds of the U.S. population. In this vast region, Customs and Border Protection (CBP) can set up checkpoints and conduct warrantless searches. At airports, American citizens are now similarly subjected to search and seizure as filmmaker Laura Poitras—whose work focuses on national security issues in general and Edward Snowden in the particular—knows firsthand. Since 2006, almost every time Poitras has returned to the U.S., her plane has been met by government agents and her laptop and phone examined.

There are multiple similar high-profile cases (including those of a Wikileaks researcher and a Chelsea Manning supporter), but ordinary citizens are hardly exempt. Despite standing in an American airport, a pane of glass away from loved ones, you are not in the U.S. and have no Fourth Amendment rights. How many such airport searches are conducted in the aggregate is unknown. The best information we have comes from a FOIA request by the ACLU. It revealed that, in the 18-month period beginning in October 2008, more than 6,600 people, about half of them U.S. citizens, were subjected to electronic device searches at the border.

Still, reminding us that it's possible to have a sense of humor on the road to hell, the CBP offers this undoubtedly inadvertent pun at its website: "It is not the intent of CBP to subject travelers to unwarranted scrutiny."

Making It All Constitutional In-House

Here's another example of how definitions have been readjusted to serve the national security state's overriding needs: the Department of Justice (DOJ) created a Post-Constitutional interpretation of the

Fourth Amendment that allows it to access millions of records of Americans using only subpoenas, not search warrants.

Some background: a warrant is court permission to search and seize something. As the Fourth Amendment makes clear, it must be specific: enter Thomas Anderson's home and look for hacked software. Warrants can only be issued on "probable cause." The Supreme Court defined probable cause as requiring a high standard of proof, or to quote its words, "a fair probability that contraband or evidence of a crime will be found in a particular place."

A subpoena on the other hand is nothing more than a government order issued to a citizen or organization to do something, most typically to produce a document. Standards for issuing a subpoena are flexible, as most executive agencies can issue them on their own without interaction with a court. In such cases, there is no independent oversight.

The Department of Justice now claims that, under the Fourth Amendment, it can simply subpoena an Internet company like Facebook and demand that they look for and turn over all the records they have on our Mr. Anderson. Their explanation: the DOJ isn't doing the searching, just demanding that another organization do it. As far as its lawyers are concerned, in such a situation, no warrant is needed. In addition, the Department of Justice believes it has the authority to subpoena multiple records, maybe even all the records Facebook has. Records on you? Some group of people including you? Everyone? We don't know, as sources of data like Facebook and Google are prohibited from disclosing much about the information they hand over to the NSA or other government outfits about you.

It's easy enough to miss the gravity of this in-house interpretation when it comes to the Fourth Amendment. If the FBI today came to your home and demanded access to your emails, it would require a warrant obtained from a court after a show of probable cause to get them. If, however, the Department of Justice can simply issue a subpoena to Google to the same end, they can potentially vacuum up every Gmail message you've ever sent without a warrant and it won't constitute a "search." The DOJ has continued this practice even though in 2010 a federal appeals court ruled that bulk warrantless access to email violates the Fourth Amendment. An FBI field manual released under the Freedom of Information Act similarly makes it clear that the Bureau's agents don't need warrants to access email in bulk when it's pulled directly from Google, Yahoo, Microsoft, or other service providers.

How far can the use of a subpoena go in bypassing the Fourth Amendment? Recently, the inspector general of the Department of Veterans Affairs (VA) issued a subpoena—no court involved—demanding that the Project On Government Oversight (POGO) turn over all information it has collected relating to abuses and mismanagement at VA medical facilities. POGO is a private, non-profit group, dedicated to assisting whistleblowers. The VA subpoena demands access to records sent via an encrypted website to POGO under a promise of anonymity, many from current or former VA employees.

Rather than seek to break the encryption surreptitiously and illegally to expose the whistleblowers, the government has taken a simpler, if unconstitutional route, by simply demanding the names and reports. POGO has refused to comply, setting up a legal confrontation. In the meantime, consider it just another sign of the direction the government is heading when it comes to the Fourth Amendment.

Technology and the Fourth Amendment

Some observers suggest that there is little new here. For example, the compiling of information on innocent Americans by J. Edgar Hoover's low-tech FBI back in the 1960s has been well documented. Paper reports on activities, recordings of conversations, and photos of meetings and trysts, all secretly obtained, exposed the lives of civil rights leaders, popular musicians, and antiwar protesters. From 1956 to at least 1971, the government also wiretapped the calls and conversations of Americans under the Bureau's counterintelligence program (COINTELPRO).

But those who look to such history of government illegality for a strange kind of nothing-new-under-the-sun reassurance have not grasped the impact of fast-developing technology. In scale, scope, and sheer efficiency, the systems now being employed inside the U.S. by the NSA and other intelligence agencies are something quite new and historically significant. Size matters.

To avoid such encroaching digitization would essentially mean withdrawing from society, not exactly an option for most Americans. More of life is now online—from banking to travel to social media. Where the NSA was once limited to traditional notions of communication—the written and spoken word— new possibilities for following you and intruding on your life in myriad ways are being created. The agency can, for instance, now collect images, photos, and video, and subject them to facial recognition technology that can increasingly put a name to a face. Such technology, employed today at casinos as well as in the secret world of the national security state, can pick out a face in a crowd and identify it, taking into account age, changes in facial hair, new glasses, hats, and the like.

An offshoot of facial recognition is the broader category of biometrics, the use of physical and biological traits unique to a person for identification. These can be anything from ordinary fingerprinting to cutting-edge DNA records and iris scans. (Biometrics is already big business and even has its own trade association in Washington.) One of the world's largest known collections of biometric data is held by the Department of State. As of December 2009, its Consular Consolidated Database (CCD) contained more than 75 million photographs of Americans and foreigners and is growing at a rate of approximately 35,000 records per day. CCD also collects and stores indefinitely the fingerprints of all foreigners issued visas.

With ever more data available, the NSA and other agencies are creating ever more robust ways to store it. Such storage is cheap and bounteous, with few limits other than the availability of electricity and water to cool the electronics. Emerging tech will surely bypass many of the existing constraints to make holding more data longer even easier and cheaper. The old days of file cabinets, or later, clunky disk drives, are over in an era of mega-data storage warehouses.

The way data is aggregated is also changing fast. Where data was once kept in cabinets in separate offices, later in bureaucratically isolated, agency-by-agency digital islands, post-9/11 sharing mandates coupled with new technology have led to fusion databases. In these, information from such disparate sources as license plate readers, wiretaps, and records of library book choices can be aggregated and easily shared. Basically everything about a person, gathered worldwide by various agencies and means, can now be put into a single "file."

Once you have the whole haystack, there's still the problem of how to locate the needle. For this, emerging technologies grow ever more capable of analyzing Big Data. Some simple ones are even available to the public, like IBM's Non-Obvious Relationship Awareness software (NORA). It can, for example, scan multiple databases, geolocation information, and social media friend lists and recognize relationships that may not be obvious at first glance. The software is fast and requires no human intervention. It runs 24/7/365/Forever.

Tools like NORA and its more sophisticated classified cousins are NSA's solution to one of the last hurdles to knowing nearly everything: the need for human analysts to "connect the dots." Skilled analysts take time to train, are prone to human error, and —given the quickly expanding supply of data—will always be in demand. Automated analysis also offers the NSA other advantages. Software doesn't have a conscience and it can't blow the whistle.

What does all this mean in terms of the Fourth Amendment? It's simple: the technological and human factors that constrained the gathering and processing of data in the past are fast disappearing. Prior to these "advances," even the most ill-intentioned government urges to intrude on and do away with the privacy of citizens were held in check by the possible. The techno-gloves are now off and the possible is increasingly whatever an official or bureaucrat wants to do. That means violations of the Fourth Amendment are held in check only by the goodwill of the government, which might have qualified as the ultimate nightmare of those who wrote the Constitution.

On this front, however, there are signs of hope that the Supreme Court may return to its check-and-balance role of the Constitutional era. One sign, directly addressing the Fourth Amendment, is this week's unanimous decision that the police cannot search the contents of a cell phone without a warrant. (The court also recently issued a ruling determining that the procedures for challenging one's inclusion on the government's no-fly list are unconstitutional, another hopeful sign.)

Prior to the cell phone decision, law enforcement held that if someone was arrested for, say, a traffic violation, the police had the right to examine the full contents of his or her cell phone—call lists, photos, social media, contacts, whatever was on the device. Police traditionally have been able to search physical objects they find on an arrestee without a warrant on the grounds that such searches are for the protection of the officers.

In its new decision, however, the court acknowledged that cell phones represent far more than a "physical object." The information they hold is a portrait of someone's life like what's in a closet at home or on a computer sitting on your desk. Searches of those locations almost always require a warrant.

Does this matter when talking about the NSA's technological dragnet? Maybe. While the Supreme Court's decision applies directly to street-level law enforcement, it does suggest an evolution within the court, a recognition of the way advances in technology have changed the Fourth Amendment. A cell phone is not an object anymore; it is now recognized as a portal to other information that a person has gathered in one place for convenience with, as of this decision, a reasonable expectation of privacy.

National Security Disclosures Under HIPPA

While the NSA's electronic basket of violations of the Fourth Amendment were, pre-Snowden, meant to take place in utter secrecy, here's a violation that sits in broad daylight: since 2002, my doctor can disclose my medical records to the NSA without my permission or knowledge. So can yours.

Congress passed the Health Information Portability and Accountability Act (HIPPA) in 1996 "to assure that individuals' health information is properly protected." You likely signed a HIPPA agreement at your doctor's office, granting access to your records. However, Congress quietly amended the HIPPA Act in 2002 to permit disclosure of those records for national security purposes. Specifically, the new version of this "privacy law" states: "We may also disclose your PHI [Personal Health Information] to authorized federal officials as necessary for national security and intelligence activities." The text is embedded deep in your health care provider's documentation. Look for it.

How does this work? We don't know. Do the NSA or other agencies have ongoing access to the medical records of all Americans? Do they have to request specific ones? Do doctors have any choice in whose records to forward under what conditions? No one knows. My HMO, after much transferring of my calls, would ultimately only refer me back to the HIPPA text with a promise that they follow the law.

The Snowden revelations are often dismissed by people who wonder what they have to hide. (Who cares if the NSA sees my cute cat videos?) That's why health-care spying stands out. How much more invasive could it be than for your government to have unfettered access to such a potentially personal and private part of your life—something, by the way, that couldn't have less to do with American "security" or combating terrorism.

Our health-care providers, in direct confrontation with the Fourth Amendment, are now part of the metastasizing national security state. You're right to be afraid, but for goodness sake, don't discuss your fears with your doctor.

How the Unreasonable Becomes Reasonable

At this point, when it comes to national security matters, the Fourth Amendment has by any practical definition been done away with as a part of Post-Constitutional America. Whole books have been written just about Edward Snowden and more information about government spying regularly becomes available. We don't lack for examples. Yet as the obviousness of what is being done becomes impossible to ignore and reassurances offered up by the president and others are shown to be lies, the government continues to spin the debate into false discussions about how to "balance" freedom versus security, to raise the specter of another 9/11 if spying is curtailed, and to fall back on that go-to "nothing to hide, nothing to fear" line.

In Post-Constitutional America, the old words that once defined our democracy are twisted in new ways, not discarded. Previously unreasonable searches become reasonable ones under new government interpretations of the Fourth Amendment. Traditional tools of law, like subpoenas and warrants, continue to exist even as they morph into monstrous new forms.

Americans are told (and often believe) that they retain rights they no longer have. Wait for the rhetoric that goes with the celebrations of our freedoms this July 4th. You won't hear a lot about the NSA then, but you should. In pre-constitutional America the colonists knew that they were under the king's thumb. In totalitarian states of the last century like the Soviet Union, people dealt with their lack of rights and privacy with grim humor and subtle protest. However, in America, ever exceptional, citizens passively watch their rights disappear in the service of dark ends, largely without protest and often while still celebrating a land that no longer exists.

The First Priority is to Protect Citizens' Rights

Onan Coca

Onan Coca is a graduate of Liberty University and earned his M.Ed. at Western Governors University in 2012.

C an I editorialize for a bit today? I know that while some of you enjoy hearing the opinion of our writers—others just want the facts, and I can appreciate that. Today, I want to ask you to hear me out, because I think that I am about to communicate an unpopular opinion to our readers and I want you to know that I say all of this from my heart and with no malice to those who disagree.

The topic is the war on terror and the debate over how we can best protect our liberties.

If you've been reading Eagle Rising for any length of time, then you probably know that I am a staunch conservative constitutionalist who believes that our nation's first duty is to protect the liberties found therein. You likely also know that I have come to loathe the politics of certain GOP leaders like Lindsey Graham (R-SC), John McCain (R-AZ) and Peter King (R-NY). For these men, the most important job of our government is to protect our citizens from danger—no matter the Constitutional cost. The desire to protect us is a noble one—but the cost is too great. In a free society we, the citizens, must be willing to take on some level of risk in an effort to secure our liberties.

This is why over the last few years I've found myself gravitating to conservatives like Rand Paul, Ted Cruz, Justin Amash, Thomas Massie, Mike Lee, Raul Labrador and others. These men are at times described as "libertarian" for their perspectives on the Constitution, but if you look at their Heritage Action scores (the

"The Fight for Liberty Is Far More Important than Security," Onan Coca, Freedom Outpost, June 9, 2015. Reprinted by permission.

conservative think tank the Heritage Foundation scores our nations representatives on a liberal to conservative scale) these men all score high on the conservative scale.

For example—Senator Rand Paul (who Graham, McCain, and others have called "left of Obama") had a *96% score* in the 112th Congress, a 93% score in the 113th, and he currently has an 82% score in the current Congress (though they've only tallied 11 votes thus far. He is consistently rated as far more conservative than many of his GOP counterparts, and yet I hear conservatives rail against Senator Paul each and every day for his foreign policy rhetoric.

I humbly ask you, dear readers, to consider the scores of Lindsey Graham, John McCain and Peter King in comparison. Folks, in the 113th Congress (2013–2014) Lindsey Graham had a rating of 47%, John McCain had a rating of 49% and Peter King had a rating of 35%!

And these liberal Republicans are somehow the men we "TRUST" on foreign policy issues? How can this be?

I'm not going to argue that Rand Paul (and the other "libertarian" Republicans) have the "right" answer on foreign policy; I only want to say that the men and women (Hillary Clinton included) leading our nation's foreign policy for the last 25 years have not done so well. So why are we considering continuing to allow them to lead us in that respect?

I would also add that the division in this debate isn't just on foreign policy, it's also on certain Constitutional questions.

On one side of the debate we have a dissenting minority saying that we must not compromise the Bill of Rights in order to fight the war on terror. On the other side we have a majority (the Graham/McCain/Obama/Clinton group) arguing that certain concessions must be made in order to ensure our safety. In response to this latter argument, can I quote the father of the Constitution, James Madison?

"Perhaps it is a universal truth that the loss of liberty at home is to be charged to provisions against danger, real or pretended, from abroad."

—James Madison, Father of the Constitution

Or perhaps you might prefer the tried and true favorite from Benjamin Franklin?

Those who would give up essential Liberty, to purchase a little temporary Safety, deserve neither Liberty nor Safety.

— Benjamin Franklin, Founding Father

Again, I don't mean to belittle the desires of those who wish to keep American citizens safe and secure. However, I do question the means of doing so.

Safety and security are important jobs of our government, but there is a reason that our founders (and some 250 years of history) held certain limitations on that power. Safety is of no use to an enslaved people. Does this sound extreme? I mean for it to.

Today, there is a cultural and political war being waged on every front in America.

- Free speech is under attack, both from the cultural fascist left who would wish to silence dissent on social issues, and from the political fascists who wish to operate in secrecy without the public knowing. Hate speech laws are becoming more popular among Democrats, and in Congress our representatives want to create new laws that would make it more difficult for freelance media (mostly internet based) to speak freely about what the government is doing. They are working hand in hand—whether by accident or on purpose matters not because the outcome is the same.

- Freedom of Religion is under pressure in a concerted effort by left-wing activists and government authorities. In many states it has become dangerous for conservative Christians to speak to the most controversial and relevant issues because of the ever present danger of being sued. In the civic and business arena things have become even more precarious as organizations which choose to take the "wrong" stand on these inflammatory cultural issues can find themselves sued by both private entities and the local government. Business owners risk everything when choosing to stick to their principles.

- Freedom of the Press is at risk, and it goes hand in hand with the threats facing free speech. The government continues to search for ways to pass media shield laws that would, instead of protecting press freedom, actually restrict it. How? The government would decide who was the "legitimate" press and who was not. For example, an internet author (or blogger) such as myself would not be considered a member of the press, so I would not have the same freedom that some traditional newspaper reporters do…even though Eagle Rising's circulation is actually far larger than most of the traditional newspaper outlets in America today. We have a mailing list of some 300,000 readers, on Facebook we reach *millions* of people each week, and yet, in the eyes of the government, our speech does not warrant the same protection as a local town newspaper with a circulation of hundreds.

- The right to bear arms is constantly under attack. For whatever reason, this is the one right that we conservatives have done a good job being vigilant in protecting. It's time we take this same kind of vigilance and use it to protect our other liberties as well.

- But the right that might be under most scrutiny today—thanks to the war on terror—is the 4th Amendment. *The right of the people to be secure in their persons, houses, papers, and effects, against unreasonable searches and seizures, shall not be violated, and no Warrants shall issue, but upon probable cause, supported by Oath or affirmation, and particularly describing the place to be searched, and the persons or things to be seized.* Whatever your stance on the NSA's mass surveillance program, whether you are for it or against it, you must realize that it stands in complete violation of the 4th Amendment. Even if the NSA were to find actionable data from the mass vacuuming of American data—the 4th Amendment strictly prohibits that information from being used in a court of law. Are we not a nation of laws? Are we not a nation of liberty?

I beg of you my dear, conservative friends to consider the ramifications if we support the NSA's warrantless mass collection of data. We are, by default, compromising the Bill of Rights and giving ammunition to those who would seek to weaken other amendments (including the 1st and the 2nd). It is incumbent upon our national security services to find ways of fighting the war on terror that do not infringe on our basic liberties ... even if it makes their jobs more difficult.

Freedom is that important.

I hope that in writing this I have not alienated any "security first" conservatives. That was not my intention. My deepest hope is only to educate and enlighten readers to another perspective—one that says, "security is important—but our liberty is more important."

CHAPTER 2

Does the Government Have the Right to Monitor Its Citizens?

Overview: Privacy Versus Security

Lee Rainie and Shiva Maniam

Lee Rainie is director of internet, science, and technology research at Pew Research Center. Shiva Maniam is a research assistant focusing on US politics and policy at Pew Research Center.

Americans have long been divided in their views about the trade-off between security needs and personal privacy. Much of the focus has been on government surveillance, though there are also significant concerns about how businesses use data. The issue flared again this week when a federal court ordered Apple to help the FBI unlock an iPhone used by one of the suspects in the terrorist attack in San Bernardino, California, in December. Apple challenged the order to try to ensure that security of other iPhones remained protected, and also to provoke a wider national conversation about how far people would like technology firms to go in protecting their privacy or cooperating with law enforcement.

Events have had a major impact on public attitudes on this issue. Terrorist attacks generate increased anxieties. For instance, the San Bernardino and Paris shootings in late 2015 had a striking impact. A Pew Research Center survey in December found that 56% of Americans were more concerned that the government's anti-terror policies have not gone far enough to protect the country, compared with 28% who expressed concern that the policies have gone too far in restricting the average person's civil liberties. Just two years earlier, amid the furor over Edward Snowden's revelations about National Security Agency surveillance programs, more said their bigger concern was that anti-terror programs had gone too far in restricting civil liberties (47%) rather than not far enough in protecting the country (35%).

"Americans Feel The Tensions Between Privacy And Security Concerns," Lee Rainie and Shiva Maniam, Fact Tank - Our Lives in Numbers, Pew Research Center, February 19, 2016. Reprinted by permission.

At the same time, there are other findings suggesting that Americans are becoming more anxious about their privacy, especially in the context of digital technologies that capture a wide array of data about them. Here is an overview of the state of play as the iPhone case moves further into legal proceedings.

How people have felt about government anti-terror policies

Pew Research Center surveys since the 9/11 terrorist attacks have generally shown that in the periods when high-profile cases related to privacy vs. security first arise, majorities of adults favor a "security first" approach to these issues, while at the same time urging that dramatic sacrifices on civil liberties be avoided. New incidents often result in Americans backing at least some extra steps by the law enforcement and intelligence communities to investigate terrorist suspects, even if that might infringe on the privacy of citizens. But many draw the line at deep interventions into their personal lives.

For instance, our survey shortly after the 9/11 attacks found that 70% of adults favored requiring citizens to carry national ID cards. At the same time, a majority balked at government monitoring of their own emails and personal phone calls or their credit card purchases.

It should be noted that surveys have also found that people's immediate concerns about security can subside over time. In a poll conducted in 2011, shortly before the 10th anniversary of 9/11, 40% said that "in order to curb terrorism in this country it will be necessary for the average person to give up some civil liberties," while 54% said it would not. A decade earlier, in the aftermath of 9/11 and before the passage of the Patriot Act, opinion was nearly the reverse (55% necessary, 35% not necessary).

When *The New York Times* reported in late 2005 that President George W. Bush authorized the NSA to eavesdrop on Americans, subsequent Pew Research Center surveys found that 50% of Americans were concerned that the government hadn't yet gone far enough in protecting the country against terrorism, and 54% said it was generally right for the government to monitor the telephone and email communications of Americans suspected of having ties with terrorists without first obtaining court permission. Some 43% said such surveillance was generally wrong. Quite similar numbers were found in a survey when President Barack Obama took office in 2009.

Right after the Snowden revelations in June 2013, a Pew Research Center poll found that 48% of Americans approved of the government's collection of telephone and internet data as part of anti-terrorism efforts. But by January 2014, approval had declined to 40%.

And many Americans continue to express concern about the government's surveillance program. In an early 2015 online survey, 52% of Americans described themselves as "very concerned" or "somewhat concerned" about government surveillance of Americans' data and electronic communications, compared with 46% who described themselves as "not very concerned" or "not at all concerned" about the surveillance.

How people feel about corporate practices

As businesses increasingly mine data about consumers, Americans are concerned about preserving their privacy when it comes to their personal information and behaviors. Those views have intensified in recent years, especially after big data breaches at companies such as Target, eBay and Anthem as well as of federal employee personnel files. Our surveys show that people now are more anxious about the security of their personal data and are more aware that greater and greater volumes of data are being collected about them. The vast majority feel they have lost control of their personal data, and this has spawned considerable anxiety. They are not very confident that companies collecting their information will keep it secure.

In assessing public attitudes, context matters —and so does how the question is framed

One consistent finding over the years about public attitudes related to privacy and societal security is that people's answers often depend on the context. The language of the questions we ask sometimes affects the way people respond.

A recent Pew Research Center study showed that, in commercial situations, people's views on the trade-off between offering information about themselves in exchange for something of value are shaped by both the conditions of the deal and the circumstances of their lives. People indicated that their interest and overall comfort level in sharing personal information depends on the company or organization with which they are bargaining and how trustworthy or safe they perceive the firm to be. It also depends on what happens to their data after they are collected, especially if the data are made available to third parties, and on how long the data are retained.

A study in the wake of the Snowden revelations showed that there was notable change in public attitudes about NSA surveillance programs when questions were modified. For instance, only 25% favored NSA surveillance when there was no mention of court approval of the program. But 37% favored it when the program was described as being approved by courts. Similarly, characterizing the government's data collection "as part of anti-terrorism efforts" garnered more support than not mentioning this (35% favored vs. 26% favored).

The Government Should Monitor its Citizens for Safety Reasons

Pew Research Center

The Pew Research Center is a nonpartisan American "fact tank" which is based in Washington, DC. It provides information on social issues, public opinion, and demographic trends shaping the United States and the world.

A majority of Americans—56%—say the National Security Agency's (NSA) program tracking the telephone records of millions of Americans is an acceptable way for the government to investigate terrorism, though a substantial minority—41%—say it is unacceptable. And while the public is more evenly divided over the government's monitoring of email and other online activities to prevent possible terrorism, these views are largely unchanged since 2002, shortly after the 9/11 terrorist attacks.

The latest national survey by the Pew Research Center and The Washington Post, conducted June 6-9 among 1,004 adults, finds no indications that last week's revelations of the government's collection of phone records and internet data have altered fundamental public views about the tradeoff between investigating possible terrorism and protecting personal privacy.

Currently 62% say it is more important for the federal government to investigate possible terrorist threats, even if that intrudes on personal privacy. Just 34% say it is more important for the government not to intrude on personal privacy, even if that limits its ability to investigate possible terrorist threats.

These opinions have changed little since an ABC News/ Washington Post survey in January 2006. Currently, there are only modest partisan differences in these opinions: 69% of Democrats

"Majority Views NSA Phone Tracking as Acceptable Anti-terror Tactic: A Pew Research Center/Washington Post Survey," Pew Research Center, June 10, 2013. Reprinted by permission.

say it is more important for the government to investigate terrorist threats, even at the expense of personal privacy, as do 62% of Republicans and 59% of independents.

However, while six-in-ten or more in older age groups say it is more important to investigate terrorism even if it intrudes on privacy, young people are divided: 51% say investigating terrorism is more important while 45% say it is more important for the government not to intrude on personal privacy, even if that limits its ability to investigate possible threats.

The survey finds that while there are apparent differences between the NSA surveillance programs under the Bush and Obama administrations, overall public reactions to both incidents are similar. Currently, 56% say it is acceptable that the NSA "has been getting secret court orders to track telephone calls of millions of Americans in an effort to investigate terrorism."

In January 2006, a few weeks after initial new reports of the Bush administration's surveillance program, 51% said it was acceptable for the NSA to investigate "people suspected of involvement with terrorism by secretly listening in on telephone calls and reading e-mails between some people in the United States and other countries, without first getting court approval to do so."

However, Republicans and Democrats have had very different views of the two operations. Today, only about half of Republicans (52%) say it is acceptable for the NSA to obtain court orders to track phone call records of millions of Americans to investigate terrorism. In January 2006, fully 75% of Republicans said it was acceptable for the NSA to investigate suspected terrorists by listening in on phone calls and reading emails without court approval.

Democrats now view the NSA's phone surveillance as acceptable by 64% to 34%. In January 2006, by a similar margin (61% to 36%), Democrats said it was unacceptable for the NSA to scrutinize phone calls and emails of suspected terrorists.

Public Divided Over Internet Monitoring

The public is divided over the government's monitoring of internet activity in order to prevent possible terrorism: 45% say the government should be able to "monitor everyone's email and other online activities if officials say this might prevent future terrorist attacks." About as many (52%) say the government should not able to do this.

These views are little changed from a July 2002 Pew Research Center survey. At that time, 45% said the government should be able to monitor everyone's internet activity if the government said it would prevent future attacks; 47% said it should not.

Young Differ on Principle, but Less on Practice

Younger Americans are more likely than older age groups to prioritize protecting personal privacy over terrorism investigations. Among people ages 18–29, 45% say it is more important for the federal government NOT to intrude on personal privacy, even if that limits its ability to investigate possible terrorist threats. That view falls to 35% among those ages 30-49 and just 27% among those ages 50 and older.

There are smaller age differences when it comes to the specific policies in the news this week. When it comes to whether the NSA tracking of phone records is acceptable, nearly the same share of 18-to-29 year-olds (55%) say the program is acceptable as those ages 65 and older (61%). Younger Americans are as divided as the nation overall about whether the government should or should not monitor email and online activities in the interest of preventing terrorism.

One-in-Four Following NSA News 'Very Closely'

Roughly a quarter (27%) of Americans say they are following news about the government collecting Verizon phone records very closely. This is a relatively modest level of public interest. Only another 21% say they are following this fairly closely, while about half say they are following not too (17%) or not at all (35%) closely.

Interest in reports about the government tracking of e-mail and online activities is almost identical: 26% say they are following this story very closely, 33% not closely at all.

As with most news stories, interest is far higher among older Americans than the young: one-in-three (33%) Americans ages 50-and-older are following news about the government tracking phone records very closely. Among those ages 18–29, just 12% are following very closely, while 56% say they are not following closely at all.

Attention to these stories is higher among Republicans and Republican-leaning independents: 32% are following reports about the government tracking phone records very closely, compared with 24% of Democrats and Democratic-leaning independents. The partisan gap in interest is almost identical when it comes to reports about government collecting email and other online information: 30% of Republicans and Republican-leaners are following very closely compared with 20% of Democrats and Democratic-leaners.

Overall, those who disagree with the government's data monitoring are following the reports somewhat more closely than those who support them. Among those who find the government's tracking of phone records to be unacceptable, 31% are following the story very closely, compared with 21% among those who say it is acceptable. Similarly with respect to reports about government monitoring of email and online activities, 28% of those who say this should not be done are following the news very closely, compared with 23% of those who approve of the practice.

About the Survey

The analysis in this report is based on telephone interviews conducted June 6–9, 2013, among a national sample of 1,004 adults 18 years of age or older living in the continental United States

(501 respondents were interviewed on a landline telephone, and 503 were interviewed on a cell phone, including 247 who had no landline telephone). The survey was conducted by interviewers at Princeton Data Source under the direction of Princeton Survey Research Associates International. A combination of landline and cell phone random digit dial samples were used; both samples were provided by Survey Sampling International. Interviews were conducted in English. Respondents in the landline sample were selected by randomly asking for the youngest adult male or female who is now at home. Interviews in the cell sample were conducted with the person who answered the phone, if that person was an adult 18 years of age or older. For detailed information about our survey methodology, see: http://www.people-press.org/methodology/.

The combined landline and cell phone sample are weighted using an iterative technique that matches gender, age, education, race, Hispanic origin and region to parameters from the 2011 Census Bureau's American Community Survey and population density to parameters from the Decennial Census. The sample also is weighted to match current patterns of telephone status, based on extrapolations from the 2012 National Health Interview Survey. The weighting procedure also accounts for the fact that respondents with both landline and cell phones have a greater probability of being included in the combined sample and adjusts for household size among respondents with a landline phone. Sampling errors and statistical tests of significance take into account the effect of weighting. The following table shows the unweighted sample sizes and the error attributable to sampling that would be expected at the 95% level of confidence for different groups in the survey:

GROUP	UNWEIGHTED SAMPLE SIZE	PLUS OR MINUS...
Total Sample	1,004	3.7 percentage points
Republicans	224	7.9 percentage points
Democrats	337	6.4 percentage points
Independents	352	6.3 percentage points
Data from Friday–Sunday interviews only	743	4.3 percentage points
Republicans	165	9.2 percentage points
Democrats	238	7.6 percentage points
Independents	273	7.1 percentage points

Sample sizes and sampling errors for other subgroups are available upon request.

In addition to sampling error, one should bear in mind that question wording and practical difficulties in conducting surveys can introduce error or bias into the findings of opinion polls.

Surveillance Is Fine, but Secrecy Isn't

Josh Stearns

Josh Stearns is a journalist and organizer. He is director of the Geraldine R. Dodge Foundation's journalism sustainability project, focused on developing new revenue models for local news rooted in community engagement and creative collaboration..

The American experiment is premised on the idea that an informed public is central to self-governance and a functioning democracy. But today, that fundamental idea is being challenged, at times by the very people—journalists and the media—who should be its staunchest defenders.

In a new post, NYU journalism professor Jay Rosen traces how the debate over Snowden and the National Security Agency has sparked what amounts to a de facto effort to "repeal the concept of an informed public." This is a critical point, and I want to draw a few more threads into the debate.

"My sole motive," Edward Snowden told the *Guardian* in his first public interview, "is to inform the public as to that which is done in their name and that which is done against them." Rosen describes Snowden as "the return of the repressed." He writes: "By going AWOL and leaking documents that show what the NSA is up to, he forced Congress to ask itself: did we really consent to that? With his disclosures the principle of an informed public roared back to life."

However, since that moment, there has been a profound effort by politicians and even some journalists to close down that debate. This opposition has taken many forms. Journalists and politicians have attacked Glenn Greenwald and tried to undercut the legitimacy of the *Guardian*. They have tried to write off NSA

"Security, Secrecy and the Democratic Demands of an Informed Public," Josh Stearns, Freedom of the Press Foundation, August 9, 2013. https://freedom.press/blog/2013/08/security-secrecy-and-democratic-demands-informed-public. Licensed under CC BY 4.0 International.

programs as balanced and well within the law. And most of all they have used fear and the threat of possible terror attacks to argue that any real debate about the details of America's surveillance programs is simply a "discussion the public cannot afford to have."

The question no one seems to be asking is what are the costs of not having that discussion—and can we afford those costs? When James Madison argued in 1822 that "A popular Government, without popular information, or the means of acquiring it, is but a Prologue to a Farce or a Tragedy; or, perhaps both," it was a warning, but it was also a choice. In the face of nearly daily revelations about the state of security and surveillance in the US it is easy to feel overwhelmed, to toss our hands up and assume the decisions being made in our name are in our interest. But inaction is also a choice. The second part of Madison's quote, "A people who mean to be their own Governors, must arm themselves with the power which knowledge gives," reminds us that too often information doesn't want to be free, we need to demand it.

Right now, the administration continues to argue they welcome this debate. But *New York Times* reporter James Risen pointed out the hypocrisy of this position this week when he said on CNN, "In Washington these days [...] people want to have debates on television and elsewhere, but then you want to throw the people who start the debates in jail." He should know, because right now the Justice Department is trying to force him to reveal his sources in a different national security leak case. If he doesn't, he'll be thrown in jail.

In 2009, concern over the changes in media and journalism sparked a landmark report from the Knight Commission on the threats and opportunities to fostering an informed public. In their opening pages the authors of the report assert that "Information is as vital to the healthy functioning of communities as clean air, safe streets, good schools and public health," and "if there is no access to information, there is a denial to citizens of an element required for participation in the life of the community." The authors challenged America and its media to:

- Maximize the availability of relevant and credible information to all Americans and their communities;
- Strengthen the capacity of individuals to engage with information; and
- Promote individual engagement with information and the public life of the community.

The Knight Commission said that their vision was driven by the "critical democratic values of openness, inclusion, participation, empowerment, and the common pursuit of truth and the public interest." Today, the challenge the Knight Commission set forth remains a useful guide as we look at the debates we face about the NSA's spying programs and the associated revelations that have spun out from these disclosures.

For too long, we've watched as government secrecy has escalated and made it more and more difficult for the public to be informed on critical issues from war and surveillance to the environment and the economy. Now we face a system so entrenched in secrecy that classifying documents is the norm in DC, the Justice Department feels empowered to monitor the phone records of journalists, states are passing Ag-Gag laws to curtail reporting and whistleblowing, and members of Congress are bold enough to suggest journalists be prosecuted for reporting the news of the day.

Mathew Ingram has even argued that "the worst part about all the government surveillance isn't the snooping, it's the secrecy." For Rosen, this secrecy forces a central question about our relationship to our government and to each other:

> Can there even be an informed public and consent-of-the-governed for decisions about electronic surveillance, or have we put those principles aside so that the state can have its freedom to maneuver?

The end result of the secrecy and the government's almost frantic efforts to protect it, is a fundamental loss of trust. That lack of trust, in our government and by extension in each other, undermines every one of the critical democratic values Knight outlined above.

In her powerful book *Talking to Strangers*, which predates the NSA controversy by almost ten years, scholar Danielle S. Allen argues:

> As for distrust of one's fellow citizens, when this pervades democratic relations, it paralyzes democracy; it means that citizens no longer think it sensible, or feel secure enough, to place their fates in the hands of democratic strangers. [...] Within democracies, such congealed distrust indicates political failure. At its best, democracy is full of contention and fluid disagreement but free of settled patterns of mutual disdain. Democracy depends on trustful talk among strangers and, properly conducted, should dissolve any divisions that block it.

For Allen, and for the Knight Commission, our security and our democracy is based on trust and openness. That's why the NSA programs aren't just a threat to the Fourth Amendment, but also the First Amendment by violating people's right of association and chilling speech. "People who make a career in journalism cannot pretend to neutrality on a matter like that," Rosen concludes. "If a free society needs them—and I think it does—it needs them to stand strongly against the eclipse of informed consent."

I couldn't agree more.

Government Is the Negation of Freedom

Andrew P. Napolitano

Andrew P. Napolitano, a former judge of the Superior Court of New Jersey, is the senior judicial analyst at Fox News Channel.

When Edward Snowden revealed that the federal government, in direct defiance of the Fourth Amendment to the Constitution, was unlawfully and unconstitutionally spying on all Americans who use telephones, text messaging or emails to communicate with other persons, he opened a Pandora's box of allegations and recriminations. The allegations he unleashed are that Americans have a government that assaults our personal freedoms, operates in secrecy and violates the Constitution and the values upon which it is based. The recriminations are that safety is a greater good than liberty, and Snowden interfered with the ability of the government to keep us safe by exposing its secrets, and so he should be silenced and punished.

In the course of this debate, you have heard the argument that we all need to sacrifice some liberty in order to assure our safety, that liberty and safety are in equipoise, and when they clash, it is the government that should balance one against the other and decide which shall prevail. This is, of course, an argument the government loves, as it presupposes that the government has the moral, legal and constitutional power to make this satanic bargain.

It doesn't.

Roman emperors and tribal chieftains, King George III and French revolutionaries, 20th-century dictators and 21st-century American presidents all have asserted that their first job is to keep us safe, and in doing so, they are somehow entitled to take away our liberties, whether it be the speech they hate or fear, the privacy

---

"Giving Up Liberty for Security," Andrew Napolitano, Reason Foundation, July 25, 2013. Reprinted by permission.

they capriciously love to invade or the private property and wealth they salaciously covet.

This argument is antithetical to the principal value upon which America was founded. That value is simply that individuals— created in the image and likeness of God and thus possessed of the freedoms that He enjoys and has shared with us—are the creators of the government. A sovereign is the source of his own powers. The government is not sovereign. All the freedom that individuals possess, we have received as a gift from God, who is the only true sovereign. All of the powers the government possesses it has received from us, from our personal repositories of freedom.

Thomas Jefferson recognized this when he wrote in the Declaration of Independence that our rights are inalienable—they cannot be separated from us—because we have been endowed with them by our Creator. James Madison, who wrote the Constitution, observed that in the history of the world, when freedom has been won, it happened because those in power begrudgingly permitted freedom as a condition of staying in power or even staying alive.

But not in America.

In America, the opposite occurred when free people voluntarily permitted the government to exercise the limited power needed to protect freedom. That is known as "the consent of the governed." To Jefferson and Madison, a government lacking that consent is illegitimate.

So, the principal author of the Declaration of Independence and the principal author of the Constitution were of one mind on this: All persons are by nature free, and to preserve those freedoms, they have consented to a government. That was the government they gave us—not power permitting liberty, but liberty permitting power —and the instrument of that permission was the Constitution.

The Constitution was created by free men to define and limit the government so it can defend but not threaten our freedoms. Since only free persons can consent to a government, the government cannot lawfully exist without those consents. Here is where the modern-day tyrants and big-government apologists have succeeded in confusing well-meaning people. They have elevated safety—which is a goal of government—to the level of freedom—which created the government. This common and pedestrian argument makes the creature—safety—equal its creator—freedom. That is a metaphysical impossibility because it presumes that the good to be purchased is somehow equal to the free choices of the purchaser.

What does this mean?

It means that when politicians say that liberty and safety need to be balanced against each other, they are philosophically, historically and constitutionally wrong. Liberty is the default position. Liberty is the essence of our natural state. Liberty cannot possibly be equal to a good we have instructed the government to obtain.

What is the only moral relationship between liberty and safety?

It cannot be balance, because liberty and safety are not equals, as one created the other. It can only be *bias*—a continual predisposition toward and preference for freedom.

Every conceivable clash between the free choices of persons and their instructions to their government to safeguard freedom must favor the free choices because freedom is inalienable. Just as I cannot authorize the government to take away your freedom any more than you can authorize it to take away mine, a majority of all but one cannot authorize the government in a free society to take freedom from that one individual. So if somehow freedom and safety do clash, it is the free choice of each person to resolve that clash for himself, and not one the government can morally make.

The government will always make choices that favor its power because, as Ludwig von Mises reminded us, government is essentially the negation of freedom. If anyone truly believes that by silencing him or monitoring him or taxing him the government keeps him safe, and that those are the least restrictive means by which to do so, let that person surrender his own speech and privacy and wealth. The rest of us will retain ours and provide for our own safety.

The reasons we have consented to limited government are to preserve the freedom to pursue happiness, the freedom to be different and the freedom to be left alone. None of these freedoms can exist if we are subservient to the government in the name of safety or anything else.

The Role of Bulk Data in Thwarting Terrorism Is Minimal

Bailey Cahall, Peter Bergen, David Sterman, and Emily Schneider

Bailey Cahall is a senior program associate in in New America's International Security Program. Peter Bergen is a print, television, and web journalist; documentary producer; and vice president at New America. David Sterman is a policy analyst in New America's International Security Program. Emily Schneider is a senior program associate in in New America's International Security Program.

On June 5, 2013, the *Guardian* broke the first story in what would become a flood of revelations regarding the extent and nature of the NSA's surveillance programs. Facing an uproar over the threat such programs posed to privacy, the Obama administration scrambled to defend them as legal and essential to U.S. national security and counterterrorism. Two weeks after the first leaks by former NSA contractor Edward Snowden were published, President Obama defended the NSA surveillance programs during a visit to Berlin, saying: "We know of at least 50 threats that have been averted because of this information not just in the United States, but, in some cases, threats here in Germany. So lives have been saved." Gen. Keith Alexander, the director of the NSA, testified before Congress that: "the information gathered from these programs provided the U.S. government with critical leads to help prevent over 50 potential terrorist events in more than 20 countries around the world." Rep. Mike Rogers (R-Mich.), chairman of the House Permanent Select Committee on Intelligence, said on the House floor in July that "54 times [the

NSA programs] stopped and thwarted terrorist attacks both here and in Europe—saving real lives."

However, our review of the government's claims about the role that NSA "bulk" surveillance of phone and email communications records has had in keeping the United States safe from terrorism shows that these claims are overblown and even misleading. An in-depth analysis of 225 individuals recruited by al-Qaeda or a like-minded group or inspired by al-Qaeda's ideology, and charged in the United States with an act of terrorism since 9/11, demonstrates that traditional investigative methods, such as the use of informants, tips from local communities, and targeted intelligence operations, provided the initial impetus for investigations in the majority of cases, while the contribution of NSA's bulk surveillance programs to these cases was minimal. Indeed, the controversial bulk collection of American telephone metadata, which includes the telephone numbers that originate and receive calls, as well as the time and date of those calls but not their content, under Section 215 of the USA PATRIOT Act, appears to have played an identifiable role in initiating, at most, 1.8 percent of these cases. NSA programs involving the surveillance of non-U.S. persons outside of the United States under Section 702 of the FISA Amendments Act played a role in 4.4 percent of the terrorism cases we examined, and NSA surveillance under an unidentified authority played a role in 1.3 percent of the cases we examined.

Regular FISA warrants not issued in connection with Section 215 or Section 702, which are the traditional means for investigating foreign persons, were used in at least 48 (21 percent) of the cases we looked at, although it's unclear whether these warrants played an initiating role or were used at a later point in the investigation.

Surveillance of American phone metadata has had no discernible impact on preventing acts of terrorism and only the most marginal of impacts on preventing terrorist-related activity, such as fundraising for a terrorist group. Furthermore, our examination of the role of the database of U.S. citizens' telephone metadata in the single plot the government uses to justify the importance of the program—that of Basaaly Moalin, a San Diego cabdriver who in 2007 and 2008 provided $8,500 to al-Shabaab, al-Qaeda's affiliate in Somalia—calls into question the necessity of the Section 215 bulk collection program. According to the government, the database of American phone metadata allows intelligence authorities to quickly circumvent the traditional burden of proof associated with criminal warrants, thus allowing them to "connect the dots" faster and prevent future 9/11-scale attacks. Yet in the Moalin case, after using the NSA's phone database to link a number in Somalia to Moalin, the FBI waited two months to begin an investigation and wiretap his phone. Although it's unclear why there was a delay between the NSA tip and the FBI wiretapping, court documents show there was a two-month period in which the FBI was not monitoring Moalin's calls, despite official statements that the bureau had Moalin's phone number and had identified him. This undercuts the government's theory that the database of Americans' telephone metadata is necessary to expedite the investigative process, since it clearly didn't expedite the process in the single case the government uses to extol its virtues.

Additionally, a careful review of three of the key terrorism cases the government has cited to defend NSA bulk surveillance programs reveals that government officials have exaggerated the role of the NSA in the cases against David Coleman Headley and Najibullah Zazi, and the significance of the threat posed by a notional plot to bomb the New York Stock Exchange.

In 28 percent of the cases we reviewed, court records and public reporting do not identify which specific methods initiated the investigation. These cases, involving 62 individuals, may have been initiated by an undercover informant, an undercover officer, a family member tip, other traditional law enforcement methods, CIA- or FBI-generated intelligence, NSA surveillance of some kind, or any number of other methods. In 23 of these 62 cases (37 percent), an informant was used. However, we were unable to determine whether the informant initiated the investigation or was used after the investigation was initiated as a result of the use of some other investigative means. Some of these cases may also be too recent to have developed a public record large enough to identify which investigative tools were used.

We have also identified three additional plots that the government has not publicly claimed as NSA successes, but in which court records and public reporting suggest the NSA had a role. However, it is not clear whether any of those three cases involved bulk surveillance programs.

Finally, the overall problem for U.S. counterterrorism officials is not that they need vaster amounts of information from the bulk surveillance programs, but that they don't sufficiently understand or widely share the information they already possess that was derived from conventional law enforcement and intelligence techniques. This was true for two of the 9/11 hijackers who were known to be in the United States before the attacks on New York and Washington, as well as with the case of Chicago resident David Coleman Headley, who helped plan the 2008 terrorist attacks in Mumbai, and it is the unfortunate pattern we have also seen in several other significant terrorism cases.

CHAPTER 3

Should Consumers Have Expectations of Privacy?

Overview: How Corporate Data Collection Affects Consumers

Timothy Morey, Theodore Forbath, and Allison Schoop

Timothy Morey is the vice president of innovation strategy at frog, a global product strategy and design firm. Theodore "Theo" Forbath is the global vice president of digital transformation at Cognizant. Allison Schoop is an associate strategy director at frog.

With the explosion of digital technologies, companies are sweeping up vast quantities of data about consumers' activities, both online and off. Feeding this trend are new smart, connected products—from fitness trackers to home systems—that gather and transmit detailed information.

Though some companies are open about their data practices, most prefer to keep consumers in the dark, choose control over sharing, and ask for forgiveness rather than permission. It's also not unusual for companies to quietly collect personal data they have no immediate use for, reasoning that it might be valuable someday.

As current and former executives at frog, a firm that helps clients create products and services that leverage users' personal data, we believe this shrouded approach to data gathering is shortsighted. Having free use of customer data may confer near-term advantages. But our research shows that consumers are aware that they're under surveillance—even though they may be poorly informed about the specific types of data collected about them—and are deeply anxious about how their personal information may be used.

In a future in which customer data will be a growing source of competitive advantage, gaining consumers' confidence will be

"Customer Data: Designing for Transparency and Trust," Timothy Morey, Theodore "Theo" Forbath, and Allison Schoop, *Harvard Business Review*, May 2015. Reprinted by permission.

key. Companies that are transparent about the information they gather, give customers control of their personal data, and offer fair value in return for it will be trusted and will earn ongoing and even expanded access. Those that conceal how they use personal data and fail to provide value for it stand to lose customers'

The Expanding Scope of Data

The internet's first personal data collectors were websites and applications. By tracking users' activities online, marketers could deliver targeted advertising and content. More recently, intelligent technology in physical products has allowed companies in many industries to collect new types of information, including users' locations and behavior. The personalization this data allows, such as constant adaptation to users' preferences, has become central to the product experience. (Google's Nest thermostat, for example, autonomously adjusts heating and cooling as it learns home owners' habits.)

The rich new streams of data have also made it possible to tackle complex challenges in fields such as health care, environmental protection, and urban planning. Take Medtronic's digital blood-glucose meter. It wirelessly connects an implanted sensor to a device that alerts patients and health care providers that blood-glucose levels are nearing troubling thresholds, allowing preemptive treatments. And the car service Uber has recently agreed to share ride-pattern data with Boston officials so that the city can improve transportation planning and prioritize road maintenance. These and countless other applications are increasing the power—and value—of personal data.

Of course, this flood of data presents enormous opportunities for abuse. Large-scale security breaches, such as the recent theft of the credit card information of 56 million Home Depot customers, expose consumers' vulnerability to malicious agents. But revelations about companies' covert activities also make consumers nervous. Target famously aroused alarm when it was revealed that the retailer used data mining to identify shoppers who were likely to be pregnant—in some cases before they'd told anyone.

At the same time, consumers appreciate that data sharing can lead to products and services that make their lives easier and more entertaining, educate them, and save them money. Neither companies nor their customers want to turn back the clock on these technologies—and indeed the development and adoption of products that leverage personal data continue to soar. The consultancy Gartner estimates that nearly 5 billion connected "things" will be in use in 2015—up 30% from 2014—and that the number will quintuple by 2020.

Resolving this tension will require companies and policy makers to move the data privacy discussion beyond advertising use and the simplistic notion that aggressive data collection is bad. We believe the answer is more nuanced guidance—specifically, guidelines that align the interests of companies and their customers, and ensure that both parties benefit from personal data collection.

Consumer Awareness and Expectations

To help companies understand consumers' attitudes about data, in 2014 we surveyed 900 people in five countries—the United States, the United Kingdom, Germany, China, and India—whose demographic mix represented the general online population. We looked at their awareness of how their data was collected and used, how they valued different types of data, their feelings about privacy, and what they expected in return for their data.

To find out whether consumers grasped what data they shared, we asked, "To the best of your knowledge, what personal information have you put online yourself, either directly or indirectly, by your use of online services?" While awareness varied by country—Indians are the most cognizant of their data trail and Germans the least—overall the survey revealed an astonishingly low recognition of the specific types of information tracked online. On average, only 25% of people knew that their data footprints included information on their location, and just 14% understood that they were sharing their web-surfing history too.

It's not as if consumers don't realize that data about them is being captured, however; 97% of the people surveyed expressed concern that businesses and the government might misuse their data. Identity theft was a top concern (cited by 84% of Chinese respondents at one end of the spectrum and 49% of Indians at the other). Privacy issues also ranked high; 80% of Germans and 72% of Americans are reluctant to share information with businesses because they "just want to maintain [their] privacy." So consumers clearly worry about their personal data—even if they don't know exactly what they're revealing.

To see how much consumers valued their data, we did conjoint analysis to determine what amount survey participants would be willing to pay to protect different types of information. (We used purchasing parity rather than exchange rates to convert all amounts to U.S. dollars.) Though the value assigned varied widely among individuals, we are able to determine, in effect, a median, by country, for each data type.

The responses revealed significant differences from country to country and from one type of data to another. Germans, for instance, place the most value on their personal data, and Chinese and Indians the least, with British and American respondents falling in the middle. Government identification, health, and credit card information tended to be the most highly valued across countries, and location and demographic information among the least.

We don't believe this spectrum represents a "maturity model," in which attitudes in a country predictably shift in a given direction over time (say, from less privacy conscious to more). Rather, our findings reflect fundamental dissimilarities among cultures. The cultures of India and China, for example, are considered more hierarchical and collectivist, while Germany, the United States, and the United Kingdom are more individualistic, which may account for their citizens' stronger feelings about personal information.

The Need to Deliver Value

If companies understand how much data is worth to consumers, they can offer commensurate value in return for it. Making the exchange transparent will be increasingly important in building trust.

A lot depends on the type of data and how the firm is going to use it. Our analysis looked at three categories: (1) *self-reported data,* or information people volunteer about themselves, such as their e-mail addresses, work and educational history, and age and gender; (2) *digital exhaust,* such as location data and browsing history, which is created when using mobile devices, web services, or other connected technologies; and (3) *profiling data,* or personal profiles used to make predictions about individuals' interests and behaviors, which are derived by combining self-reported, digital exhaust, and other data. Our research shows that people value self-reported data the least, digital exhaust more, and profiling data the most.

We also examined three categories of data use: (1) *making a product or service better,* for example, by allowing a map application to recommend a route based on a user's location; (2) *facilitating targeted marketing or advertising,* such as ads based on a user's browsing history; and (3) *generating revenues through resale,* by, say, selling credit card purchase data to third parties.

Our surveys reveal that when data is used to improve a product or service, consumers generally feel the enhancement itself is a fair trade for their data. But consumers expect more value in return for data used to target marketing, and the most value for data that will be sold to third parties. In other words, the value consumers place on their data rises as its sensitivity and breadth increase from basic information that is voluntarily shared to detailed information about the consumer that the firm derives through analytics, and as its uses go from principally benefiting the consumer (in the form of product improvements) to principally benefiting the firm (in the form of revenues from selling data).

Let's look now at how some companies manage this trade-off.

Samsung's Galaxy V smartphone uses digital exhaust to automatically add the contacts users call most to a favorites list. Most customers value the convenience enough to opt in to the feature— effectively agreeing to swap data for enhanced performance.

Google's predictive application Google Now harnesses profiling data to create an automated virtual assistant for consumers. By sifting through users' e-mail, location, calendar, and other data, Google Now can, say, notify users when they need to leave the office to get across town for a meeting and provide a map for their commute. The app depends on more-valuable types of personal data but improves performance enough that many users willingly share it. Our global survey of consumers' attitudes toward predictive applications finds that about two-thirds of people are willing (and in some cases eager) to share data in exchange for their benefits.

Disney likewise uses profiling data gathered by its MagicBand bracelet to enhance customers' theme park and hotel experiences and create targeted marketing. By holding the MagicBand up to sensors around Disney facilities, wearers can access parks, check in at reserved attractions, unlock their hotel doors, and charge food and merchandise. Users hand over a lot of data, but they get convenience and a sense of privileged access in return, making the trade-off worthwhile. Consumers know exactly what they're signing on for, because Disney clearly spells out its data collection policies in its online MagicBand registration process, highlighting links to FAQs and other information about privacy and security.

Firms that sell personal information to third parties, however, have a particularly high bar to clear, because consumers expect the most value for such use of their data. The personal finance website Mint makes this elegant exchange: If a customer uses a credit card abroad and incurs foreign transaction fees, Mint flags the fees and refers the customer to a card that doesn't charge them. Mint receives a commission for the referral from the new-card issuer, and the customer avoids future fees. Mint and its customers both collect value from the deal.

Trust and Transparency

Firms may earn access to consumers' data by offering value in return, but trust is an essential facilitator, our research shows. The more trusted a brand is, the more willing consumers are to share their data.

Numerous studies have found that transparency about the use and protection of consumers' data reinforces trust. To assess this effect ourselves, we surveyed consumers about 46 companies representing seven categories of business around the world. We asked them to rate the firms on the following scale: *completely trustworthy* (respondents would freely share sensitive personal data with a firm because they trust the firm not to misuse it); *trustworthy* (they would "not mind" exchanging sensitive data for a desired service); *untrustworthy* (they would provide sensitive data only if required to do so in exchange for an essential service); and *completely untrustworthy* (they would never share sensitive data with the firm).

After primary care doctors, new finance firms such as PayPal and China's Alipay received the highest ratings on this scale, followed by e-commerce companies, consumer electronics makers, banks and insurance companies, and telecommunications carriers. Next came internet leaders (such as Google and Yahoo) and the government. Ranked below these organizations were retailers and entertainment companies, with social networks like Facebook coming in last.

A firm that is considered untrustworthy will find it difficult or impossible to collect certain types of data, regardless of the value offered in exchange. Highly trusted firms, on the other hand, may be able to collect it simply by asking, because customers are satisfied with past benefits received and confident the company will guard their data. In practical terms, this means that if two firms offer the same value in exchange for certain data, the firm with the higher trust will find customers more willing to share. For example, if Amazon and Facebook both wanted to launch a mobile wallet service, Amazon, which received good ratings in our survey, would meet with more customer acceptance than Facebook, which had low ratings. In this equation, trust could be an important competitive differentiator for Amazon.

Approaches That Build Trust

Many have argued that the extensive data collection today's business models rely on is fraught with security, financial, and brand risks. MIT's Sandy Pentland and others have proposed principles and practices that would give consumers a clear view of their data and control over its use, reducing firms' risks in the process.

We agree that these business models are perilous and that risk reduction is essential. And we believe reasoned policies governing data use are important. But firms must also take the lead in educating consumers about their personal data. Any firm that thinks it's sufficient to simply provide disclosures in an end-user licensing agreement or present the terms and conditions of data use at sign-up is missing the point. Such moves may address regulatory requirements, but they do little if anything to help consumers.

Consider the belated trust-building efforts under way at Facebook. The firm has been accused of riding roughshod over user privacy in the past, launching services that pushed the boundaries on personal data use and retreating only in the face of public backlash or the threat of litigation. Facebook Beacon, which exposed users' web activities without their permission or knowledge, for example, was pulled only after a barrage of public criticism.

More recently, however, Facebook has increased its focus on safeguarding privacy, educating users, and giving them control. It grasps that trust is no longer just "nice to have." Commenting in a Wired interview on plans to improve Facebook Login, which allows users to log into third-party apps with their Facebook credentials, CEO Mark Zuckerberg explained that "to get to the next level and become more ubiquitous, [Facebook Login] needs to be trusted even more. We're a bigger company now and people have more questions. We need to give people more control over their information so that everyone feels comfortable using these products." In January 2015 Facebook launched Privacy Basics, an easy-to-understand site that explains what others see about a user and how people can customize and manage others' activities on their pages.

Like Facebook, Apple has had its share of data privacy and security challenges—most recently when celebrity iPhoto accounts were hacked—and is taking those concerns ever more seriously. Particularly as Apple forays into mobile payments and watch-based fitness monitoring, consumer trust in its data handling will be paramount. CEO Tim Cook clearly understands this. Launching a "bid to be conspicuously transparent," as the Telegraph put it, Apple recently introduced a new section on its website devoted to data security and privacy. At the top is a message from Cook. "At Apple, your trust means everything to us," he writes. "That's why we respect your privacy and protect it with strong encryption, plus strict policies that govern how all data is handled....We believe in telling you up front exactly what's going to happen to your personal information and asking for your permission before you share it with us."

On the site, Apple describes the steps taken to keep people's location, communication, browsing, health tracking, and transactions private. Cook explains, "Our business model is very straightforward: We sell great products. We don't build a profile based on your email content or web browsing habits to sell to advertisers. We don't 'monetize' the information you store on your iPhone or in iCloud. And we don't read your email or your messages to get information to market to you. Our software and services are designed to make our devices better. Plain and simple." Its new stance earned Apple the highest possible score—six stars— from the nonprofit digital rights organization Electronic Frontier Foundation, a major improvement over its 2013 score of one star.

Enlightened Data Principles

Facebook and Apple are taking steps in the right direction but are fixing issues that shouldn't have arisen in the first place. Firms in that situation start the trust-building process with a handicap. Forward-looking companies, in contrast, are incorporating data privacy and security considerations into product development from the start, following three principles. The examples below each highlight one principle, but ideally companies should practice all three.

Teach your customers.

Users can't trust you if they don't understand what you're up to. Consider how one of our clients educates consumers about its use of highly sensitive personal data.

This client, an information exchange for biomedical researchers, compiles genomic data on anonymous participants from the general public. Like all health information, such data is highly sensitive and closely guarded. Building trust with participants at the outset is essential. So the project has made education and informed consent central to their experience. Before receiving a kit for collecting a saliva sample for analysis, volunteers must watch a video about the potential consequences of having their genome sequenced—including the possibility of discrimination in employment and insurance—and after viewing it, must give a preliminary online consent to the process. The kit contains a more detailed hard-copy agreement that, once signed and returned with the sample, allows the exchange to include the participant's anonymized genomic information in the database. If a participant returns the sample without the signed consent, her data is withheld from the exchange. Participants can change their minds at any time, revoking or granting access to their data.

Give them control.

The principle of building control into data exchange is even more fully developed in another project, the Metadistretti e-monitor, a collaboration between frog, Flextronics, the University Politecnico di Milano, and other partners. Participating cardiac patients wear an e-monitor, which collects ECG data and transmits it via smartphone to medical professionals and other caregivers. The patients see all their own data and control how much data goes to whom, using a browser and an app. They can set up networks of health care providers, of family and friends, or of fellow users and patients, and send each different information. This patient-directed approach is a radical departure from the tradition of paternalistic medicine that carries over to many medical devices even today, with which the patient doesn't own his data or even have access to it.

Deliver in-kind value.

Businesses needn't pay users for data (in fact, our research suggests that offers to do so actually reduce consumers' trust). But as we've discussed, firms do have to give users value in return.

The music service Pandora was built on this principle. Pandora transparently gathers self-reported data; customers volunteer their age, gender, and zip code when they sign up, and as they use the service they tag the songs they like or don't like. Pandora takes that information and develops a profile of each person's musical tastes so that it can tailor the selection of songs streamed to him or her; the more data users provide, the better the tailoring becomes. In the free version of its service, Pandora uses that data to target advertising. Customers get music they enjoy at no charge and ads that are more relevant to them. Consumers clearly find the trade satisfactory; the free service has 80 million active subscribers.

In designing its service, Pandora understood that customers are most willing to share data when they know what value they'll receive in return. It's hard to set up this exchange gracefully, but one effective approach is to start slowly, asking for a few pieces of low-value data that can be used to improve a service. Provided that there's a clear link between the data collected and the enhancements delivered, customers will become more comfortable sharing additional data as they grow more familiar with the service.

If your company still needs another reason to pursue the data principles we've described, consider this: Countries around the world are clamping down on businesses' freewheeling approach to personal data.

There is an opportunity for companies in this defining moment. They can abide by local rules only as required, or they can help lead the change under way. Grudging and minimal compliance may keep a firm out of trouble but will do little to gain consumers' trust—and may even undermine it. Voluntarily identifying and adopting the most stringent data privacy policies will inoculate a firm against legal challenges and send consumers an important message that helps confer competitive advantage. After all, in an information economy, access to data is critical, and consumer trust is the key that will unlock it.

Young People Oppose Online Surveillance

Tatsuhei Morozumi **and Marie** *Wachinger*

Tatsuhei Morozumi and Marie Wachinger are contributors to Youthpolicy.org.

> Especially for the younger generation, the Internet is not some standalone, separate domain where a few of life's functions are carried out. It is not merely our post office and our telephone. Rather, it is the epicenter of our world, the place where virtually everything is done. It is where friends are made, where books and films are chosen, where political activism is organized, where the most private data is created and stored. It is where we develop and express our very personality and sense of self.
>
> – Glenn Greenwald: "No Place to Hide: Edward Snowden, the NSA, and the U.S. Surveillance State"

A ccording to a survey conducted by the UNESCO, the number of Internet users doubled between 2005 and 2011. In 2011, 30.2% of the world's population had access to the Internet, compared to only 0.4% in 1995. Estimates are that by 2020, between four and five billion people will use the Internet—well over 50% of the world's population. Young people aged 15–34, who make up 33.05% of the global population, currently account for the majority of Internet users.

For most, the Internet is an essential tool associated with great advantages and opportunities. However, there is a growing movement of consciousness about the dangers and threats arising out of the use of the Internet, particularly the way in which personal data is harvested and exploited.

A growing consciousness

Between May 6–8th 2014, more than five thousand digital activists from all over the world gathered at Re:publica in Berlin. Originally set up as a meet-up for bloggers in 2008, Re:publica has since become one of the most important events for activists to debate developments in the digital commons. Prominent at this year's gathering were the themes of Internet privacy, and what has been dubbed a "'golden age of mass surveillance"—particularly framed within Edward Snowden's revelations on the nature and extent of NSA surveillance.

Within this context, young people are confronted with an impossible situation to navigate: on the one hand, they are growing up in a highly technologically connected society in which online presence is a pre-requisite. On the other, they have limited political control over the corporations such as Google and Facebook, who wish to profit from their data, and governments who are increasingly seeking to access this data and control the online environment.

Frequently, concerns about privacy and surveillance are rebuffed with the repost, "If you have nothing to hide, you have nothing to fear".

So are concerns about a loss of privacy and mass surveillance by corporations and the state something that youth should fear?

Freedom, security and democracy

Although the globalised world is facing challenges that justify—and possibly even require—some degree of surveillance, the NSA revelations have shown that some governments do not merely use such technological tools for prosecution, but actually have a very complete picture of all citizens' communication, or at least the means and infrastructure to get it at any stage.

History should have taught us a lesson about the dangers associated with surveillance. Repeatedly, repressive governments have used and continue to use private information of citizens to silence, persecute and oppress their critics. At Re:publica, Katja Gloger, a journalist and member of Reporters Without Borders, noted:

> What the NSA can do technically can be brought to perfection in repressive political systems. And software products from countries like Germany are being exported to authoritarian regimes, which leads to the repression and torture of journalists.

But it is not just stereotypically authoritarian regimes that are engaged in this activity, governments in the West are spying extensively on their own citizens. Glenn Greenwald (2014) argues that:

> It is not hard to understand why authorities in United States and other Western nations have been tempted to construct a ubiquitous system of spying directed at their own citizens. Worsening economic inequality, converted into a full-blown crisis by the financial collapse in 2008, has generated grave internal instability... Authorities faced with unrest generally have two options: to placate the population with symbolic concessions or fortify their interests. Elites in the West seem to view the second option—fortifying their power—as their better, perhaps only viable course of action to protect their position.
>
> – "No Place to Hide: Edward Snowden, the NSA, and the U.S. Surveillance State"

Glenn Greenwald also argues that the ubiquitous surveillance systems not only oppress and restrict organising movements or protests, but also kill the dissent in peoples' minds. At the heart of the struggle of the Internet lie the same concerns that have been raised in recent youth-led protest movements. If we do not manage to control the mass surveillance and make use of technologies responsibly, the stability and legitimacy of democracies as political systems is at stake. The real question is: How much surveillance can democracy withstand?

The political and legislative environment

The legal implications of this mass surveillance were touched upon by another prominent and notable keynote speaker—Sarah Harrison from Wikileaks, who helped Snowden escape from the U.S, authorities and advised him to stay in Russia. She personally left the U.K. to move to Berlin at the end of last year after her lawyer recommended she should not return home because of the U.K.'s anti-terror laws.

Harrison stressed the depth and scale of the intelligence activity by NSA and called for an international treaty, which demands countries to grant asylum to whistle-blowers. She further mentioned the German government's unwillingness to grant Snowden asylum and stressed the urgency of the situation, appealing to the Re:publica audience: "You have two months to sort your government out, folks!"

In fact, the legal protection for whistle-blowers is very limited. Transparency International reported that only four countries (Luxembourg, Romania, Slovenia and U.K.) hold "comprehensive or near comprehensive" legal frameworks for disclosures. This report was composed after the European Commission rejected the proposal of a law on the protection of whistle-blowers at the end of the last year.

The (lack of) legal protection of Edward Snowden is the best example to show how politicians have no desire to reveal their involvement, not to mention stopping it. Harrison condemns the treatment of whistle-blowers, explaining that, "the concept that information itself can cause harm is not logical. Actually leaked documents have enabled people to get justice." And this is where Harrison brings the topic to the core of our political systems:

Governments keep everything private, but then collect all information about us, whilst it should be the other way round.

Christian Flisek from the German Social Democrats (SPD) believes that the recent developments will eventually cause structural change. "Code is Law," he explains, "making those who master the code a substitute for legislators."

Youth attitudes, youth action

In light of the unwillingness and inability of governments to regulate this environment, responsibility for managing which companies can harvest your data is shifted to the individual.

Attitudes suggest a growing critical awareness—according to the European Youth Poll, which surveyed young people aged between 16 and 27 from 43 European countries, 62.3% disagreed with the justification of mass surveillance for the sake of the fight against terrorism. Moreover, 83.4% of youth answered, "I strongly disagree" and "I somewhat disagree" to the question "My government is doing enough to reveal the extent of the mass surveillance programs to the public." Young people, by 60% to 34%, think that the NSA leak serves the public interest.

These attitudes have started to result in behaviour changes amongst young people. After Snowden's revelations, demand for anonymous web services increased. For instance, DuckDuckGo is a search engine that enables people to surf on the Internet anonymously. DuckDuckGo's use skyrocketed after the series of disclosures about the NSA and became a popular alternative to Google.

Another anonymous search engine is Startpage, which currently handles 3 million searches a day. Similarly, the use of OTR (Off the Record) chat message apps that use end-to-end encryption such as Threema and Telegram has increased exponentially as people have sought to switch away from Whatsapp following security concerns and its acquisition by Facebook. However, the market share of these services is tiny in comparison to other high profile services, which are rapidly expanding their data harvesting services across the globe. Myshadow.org is a web page that helps to visualize your trace on the internet and informs about useful tools to help you defend your privacy.

Although a majority of young people sympathise with Edward Snowden, and many are developing a critical attitude towards data surveillance, political pressure to truly stop the limitless scanning of data is not high enough. Too many of us rely habitually on the convenience of increasingly monopolistic Internet services, despite them exploiting and profiting from our data.

Maybe attractive and easy-to-use, safe alternatives to services like Gmail and Facebook in combination with increased awareness can change this, but they need to come fast. We are already close to being "humans made from glass," as a German metaphor describes it. Redressing the balance will take a combination of individual behaviour change and political pressure to strengthen legislation.

A way forward

Many European politicians now acknowledge the necessity for protecting privacy, reconsidering the relations with U.S-based services and policies, and prepare for a data protection act in Europe. But does this mean young people—those generations that grew up with the internet—are sufficiently involved in the political decision making about internet governance?

A few initiatives are taking first steps. For instance, NERDY is a relatively new network initiated by a group of young activists and international youth organisations who felt that it was time to get involved in how the digital future is being shaped. Another example is the Youth @ EuroDig 2014 which took place in Berlin in June, hosting a session about young people and Internet governance.

Glenn Greenwald described the Internet as "the epicentre of our world." It is remarkable how true this is for young peoples' social lives, and how untrue for the political decision-making. But we are left wondering three things:

- When will serious steps be taken towards regulating the data harvesting by monopolistic corporations?
- How will communication, especially of young people, be protected?
- Or do we have to accept that there is no such thing as online privacy?

We Need Stronger Laws to Protect Data from Government and Corporations

Ethical Consumer

Ethical Consumer *rates products and companies to help consumers make wise, ethical buying choices.*

For over a year now the media has been publishing documents released by Edward Snowden, a former contractor of the National Security Agency (NSA), the communications interception specialist intelligence agency of the United States.

The Snowden files, which continue to be drip fed to news agencies such as the Guardian, reveal a number of mass surveillance programmes undertaken by the NSA and its British counterpart the Government Communications Headquarters (GCHQ).

The revelations lay bare the agencies' ability and willingness to access information stored by the major internet companies as well as mass-intercept data from fibre optic cables which make up the backbone of global phone and internet networks.

The situation has raised a number of concerns, not least the scale of global monitoring of the communications technology sector and the extent to which private companies, including many popular consumer brands, are cooperating with intelligence agencies. The extent of corporate complicity is, however, still a matter for debate.

Many of the companies implicated in the Snowden files (or that have colluded with oppressive regimes in order to operate in those markets) have taken a public policy position opposing mass surveillance, aimed at regaining the trust of their customers.

Google boss Larry Page and Facebook co-founder Mark Zuckerberg have both denied co-operatingwith NSA surveillance programmes such as PRISM.

"State Surveillance & Corporate Complicity." *Ethical Consumer*, September 2014. Reprinted by permission.

Page claimed:

> We have not joined any program that would give the US government or any other government direct access to our servers.

In a public Facebook message, Zuckerberg said:

> We have never received a blanket request or court order from any government agency asking for information or metadata in bulk…and if we did, we would fight it aggressively… We strongly encourage all governments to be much more transparent about all programs aimed at keeping the public safe.

Snowden has also criticised Amazon, who were notable by their absence from any of the PRISM documents, for "leaking info like a sieve". At a recent conference Snowden explained that intelligence agencies are currently able to monitor whatever you read on the Amazon website, and asked why the company was failing to implement proper website encryption.

In August 2013 a French consumer rights group named Google and other internet companies as potential accomplices to the NSA and FBI. The prosecutor's office in Paris has now launched a preliminary investigation into the companies' complicity with the PRISM surveillance programme.

The issues for consumers

Anna Fielder, Chair of Privacy International, believes that the big issue for consumers is that they are no longer in control of their personal information. She says the biggest areas of contention are automated profiling and the transfer of personal data.

Automated profiling is the collection and use of pieces of information about individuals to make assumptions about them and their future behaviour. This can, of course, be done by corporations and governments alike.

Anna told Ethical Consumer:

> We have to ask ourselves: "Has it gone too far?" In the age of infinite data collection (so-called big data) and hundreds of databases holding personal information, disparate pieces of

information can be combined and recombined to produce new information about you, more than you would know yourself. Profiling is likely to perpetuate and reinforce societal inequality, so it must be carefully monitored.

Legal action by Privacy International and others has forced an admission from the British government of a secret policy for mass surveillance of residents' Facebook and Google use. Britain's top counter-terrorism official has claimed that the indiscriminate interception of these communications is legal as they are "external communications" which use web-based platforms based in the US.[2]

In regard to the transfer of your personal data to third countries, Anna told us, "as most of the mass market internet corporations are US companies (Google, Facebook, Amazon, etc.), we are talking really about transfers to the US which has very weak data protection laws. There's an agreement between the UK and USA on data transfers—called Safe Harbor—but it's not very safe. It's voluntary, companies cheat and it has not been enforced properly."

Transparency initiatives

The best information we have at the moment about state monitoring of internet communications is from voluntary company transparency initiatives. Under pressure from organisations such as the Electronic Frontier Foundation, a privacy watchdog group, companies are now beginning to produce transparency reports in order to reassure consumers and be seen to do the right thing.

The mobile phone network provider Vodafone's first transparency report, released in June, was the first to cover a global dataset. It made grim reading and demonstrated the extent to which corporations and states are colluding.

The company admitted that in six of the 29 countries where it operates, governments enjoy direct access to communications on its network. In some countries police have a direct link to customers' phone calls and web communications and no warrant to intercept communications is needed. Human rights organisation Liberty called the government powers "terrifying".

The report also gave a breakdown of lawful intercept requests and communications data requests for the 29 countries in which Vodafone operates. Italy made 139,962 interception requests in total and 605,601 communications requests to Vodafone alone. By comparison the UK government made 2,760 interception requests and 514,608 communications data requests to all mobile phone operators in 2013.[1]

Internet giant Facebook reported earlier this year that it received requests from governments and courts around the world about over 70,000 users in 2013. The United States counts for 50% of these requests. The vast majority were related to criminal cases and were made by government officials as part of official investigations. Facebook also received 10,000 requests by agencies such as the NSA and the Federal Bureau of Investigation (FBI). These requests usually regard investigation "to protect against international terrorism or clandestine intelligence activities."[3]

According to the project "Silk" a transparency reports database, the number of inquiries that governments globally have submitted to the major telecommunication and internet companies of the western world amounted to more than 828,000 requests for users' data in 2013.

The United States is the world's most inquisitive country by a big margin, with over 730,000 requests, which corresponds to 3,000 requests for each million of the country's internet users. It is followed by Australia (47,000 requests), Germany (30,000 requests), France (22,000 requests) and the United Kingdom (10,000 requests).

Some of these requests have been coming from countries with dubious democratic standards. For example, Turkey submitted 12,000 data requests to companies when protests in Turkey started to escalate in 2013. The Turkish government responded with arrests of journalists and attempts to shut down social media outlets.

Microsoft complied with 76% of Turkey's requests. No other company contacted by Turkey complied with the exception of Facebook (which complied with 47%).[4]

The numbers outlined in the various transparency reports are the tip of the iceberg because the reports only contain the requests that authorities file through standard legal procedures, thus excluding data collected through bulk surveillance programmes and unauthorized interceptions, like the NSA's or GCHQ's.

Smaller companies fighting back

However, the security services and big business are clearly not having it all their own way. The release of PRISM files represented the first step in a fight back against the surveillance state and a loss of privacy.

Several smaller alternative Internet Service Providers (ISPs) from around the world have used the information released by Snowden to lodge formal complaints against GCHQ alleging it uses malicious software to break into their networks.

The claims come from seven organisations based in six countries, including our Best Buy ISP GreenNet and popular activist ISP the Riseup Collective.

The claims are being filed with the investigatory powers tribunal (IPT), a court in London that assesses complaints about the agencies' activities and the misuse of surveillance by government organisations.

The complaint is based on allegations that GCHQ carried out an attack, codenamed Operation Socialist, on the Belgian telecoms group Belgacom, whose customers include the European Commission and Parliament.

Cedric Knight of GreenNet said in a statement: "Our long-established network of NGOs and charities, or simply individuals who value our independent and ethical standpoint, rely on us for a level of integrity they can't get from mainstream ISPs. Our entire modus operandi is threatened by this illegal and intrusive mass surveillance."

What can you do

Anna from Privacy International says that the message to consumers in the short term is simple: "Switch away from US corporations providing services.... [move] away from Gmail or Hotmail to one of the very many EU-based email providers. It won't protect you from GCHQ, but at least you have stronger data protection laws."

However, she is also clear that there needs to be reform on a policy and legal level. "There are some quick or short term solutions that consumers can take, but ultimately data protection laws need to be strengthened, and the only way that can happen is through political will. Demand that your elected representatives take these issues seriously."

References

1. www.vodafone.com/content/sustainabilityreport/2014/index/operating_responsibly/privacy_and_security/law_enforcement.html
2. www.privacyinternational.org/press-releases/uk-intelligence-forced-to-reveal-secret-policy-for-mass-surveillance-of-residents
3. www.rt.com/usa/doj-reviews-fbi-surveillance-468
4. www.transparency-reports.silk.co

The Coming "Internet of Things" Will Have a Dark Side

Catherine Crump and Matthew Harwood

Catherine Crump is a staff attorney with the ACLU's Speech, Privacy and Technology Project. Matthew Harwood is senior writer/editor and media strategist for the ACLU.

E stimates vary, but by 2020 there could be over 30 billion devices connected to the Internet. Once dumb, they will have smartened up thanks to sensors and other technologies embedded in them and, thanks to your machines, your life will quite literally have gone online.

The implications are revolutionary. Your smart refrigerator will keep an inventory of food items, noting when they go bad. Your smart thermostat will learn your habits and adjust the temperature to your liking. Smart lights will illuminate dangerous parking garages, even as they keep an "eye" out for suspicious activity.

Techno-evangelists have a nice catchphrase for this future utopia of machines and the never-ending stream of information, known as Big Data, it produces: the Internet of Things. So abstract. So inoffensive. Ultimately, so meaningless.

A future Internet of Things does have the potential to offer real benefits, but the dark side of that seemingly shiny coin is this: companies will increasingly know all there is to know about you. Most people are already aware that virtually everything a typical person does on the Internet is tracked. In the not-too-distant future, however, real space will be increasingly like cyberspace, thanks to our headlong rush toward that Internet of Things. With the rise of the networked device, what people do in their homes, in their cars, in stores, and within their communities will be monitored and analyzed in ever more intrusive ways by corporations and, by extension, the government.

And one more thing: in cyberspace it is at least theoretically possible to log off. In your own well-wired home, there will be no "opt out."

You can almost hear the ominous narrator's voice from an old "Twilight Zone" episode saying, "Soon the net will close around all of us. There will be no escape."

Except it's no longer science fiction. It's our barely distant present.

Home Invasion

"[W]e estimate that only one percent of things that could have an IP address do have an IP address today, so we like to say that ninety-nine percent of the world is still asleep," Padmasree Warrior, Cisco's Chief Technology and Strategy Officer, told the Silicon Valley Summit in December. "It's up to our imaginations to figure out what will happen when the ninety-nine percent wakes up."

Yes, imagine it. Welcome to a world where everything you do is collected, stored, analyzed, and, more often than not, packaged and sold to strangers—including government agencies.

In January, Google announced its $3.2 billion purchase of Nest, a company that manufactures intelligent smoke detectors and thermostats. The signal couldn't be clearer. Google believes Nest's vision of the "conscious home" will prove profitable indeed. And there's no denying how cool the technology is. Nest's smoke detector, for instance, can differentiate between burnt toast and true danger. In the wee hours, it will conveniently shine its nightlight as you groggily shuffle to the toilet. It speaks rather than beeps. If there's a problem, it can contact the fire department.

The fact that these technologies are so cool and potentially useful shouldn't, however, blind us to their invasiveness as they operate 24/7, silently gathering data on everything we do. Will companies even tell consumers what information they're gathering? Will consumers have the ability to determine what they're comfortable with? Will companies sell or share data gathered from your home to third parties? And how will companies protect that data from hackers and other miscreants?

The dangers aren't theoretical. In November, the British tech blogger Doctorbeet discovered that his new LG Smart TV was snooping on him. Every time he changed the channel, his activity was logged and transmitted unencrypted to LG. Doctorbeet checked the TV's option screen and found that the setting "collection of watching info" was turned on by default. Being a techie, he turned it off, but it didn't matter. The information continued to flow to the company anyway.

As more and more household devices—your television, your thermostat, your refrigerator—connect to the Internet, device manufacturers will undoubtedly follow a model of comprehensive data collection and possibly infinite storage. (And don't count on them offering you an opt-out either.) They have seen the giants of the online world—the Googles, the Facebooks—make money off their users' personal data and they want a cut of the spoils. Your home will know your secrets, and chances are it will have loose lips.

The result: more and more of what happens behind closed doors will be open to scrutiny by parties you would never invite into your home. After all, the Drug Enforcement Administration already subpoenas utility company records to determine if electricity consumption in specific homes is consistent with a marijuana-growing operation. What will come next? Will eating habits collected by smart fridges be repackaged and sold to healthcare or insurance companies as predictors of obesity or other health problems—and so a reasonable basis for determining premiums? Will smart lights inform drug companies of insomniac owners?

Keep in mind that when such data flows are being scrutinized, you'll no longer be able to pull down the shades, not when the Peeping Toms of the twenty-first century come packaged in glossy, alluring boxes. Many people will just be doing what Americans have always done—upgrading their appliances. It may not initially dawn on them that they are also installing surveillance equipment targeted at them. And companies have obvious incentives to obscure this fact as much as possible.

As the "conscious home" becomes a reality, we will all have to make a crucial and conscious decision for ourselves: Will I let this device into my home? Renters may not have that option. And eventually there may only be internet-enabled appliances.

Commercial Stalking

The minute you leave your home, the ability to avoid surveillance technologies masquerading as something else will, if anything, lessen.

Physical sensors connected to the Internet are increasingly everywhere, ready to detect a unique identifier associated with you, usually one generated by your smartphone, then log what you do and leverage the data you generate for insight into your life. For instance, Apple introduced iBeacon last year. It's a service based on transmitters that employ Bluetooth technology to track where Apple users are in stores and restaurants. (The company conveniently turned on Bluetooth by default via a software update it delivered to Apple iPhone owners.) Apps that use iBeacon harvest a user's data, including his or her location, and sometimes can even turn on a device's microphone to listen in on what's going on.

Another company, Turnstyle Solutions Inc., has placed sensors around Toronto that surreptitiously record signals emitted by WiFi-enabled devices and can track users' movements. Turnstyle can tell, for instance, when a person who visited a restaurant goes to a bar or a hotel. When people log-on to WiFi networks Turnstyle has installed at area restaurants or coffee shops and check Facebook, the company can go far beyond location, collecting "names, ages, genders, and social media profiles," according to the *Wall Street Journal*.

The rationale for apps that track where you are is that business owners can use the data to tailor the customer experience to your liking. If you're wandering around the male grooming section of a particular retailer, the store could shoot you a coupon to convince you to purchase that full body trimmer that promises a smooth shave every time. If customers enter Macy's and zig right more often than left, the store can strategically place what's popular or on sale in those high-traffic areas. This is basically what's happening online now, and brick and mortar stores want in so they can compete against the Amazons of the world.

Not so surprisingly, however, such handy technology has already led to discriminatory behavior by retailers. About a year ago, an investigation by the *Wall Street Journal* found that prices quoted by online retailers like Staples and Home Depot changed based on who the customer was. People who lived in higher-income areas generally received the best deals, which is a form of digital redlining. In the future, count on brick and mortar stores to do the same thing by identifying your phone, picking up data about you, and pricing items according to just how juicy a customer they think you may be.

To be able to do this, retailers need companies that can provide rich data about our lives. That's where a group of pioneering companies in the new universe of customer surveillance called data aggregators come in. Already a multibillion-dollar industry, aggregators like Acxiom, Experian, and Datalogix buy customer data from wherever they can—banks, travel websites, retailers— and turn it into Big Data. Then they analyze, package, and sell it to third parties. "Our digital reach," said Scott Howe, CEO of the largest data aggregator, Acxiom, "will soon approach nearly every Internet user in the U.S."

Last December, the Senate Commerce Committee investigated the business practices of the nine largest data aggregators: what information they collect, how they obtain it, their invasiveness, and who they sell it to. The committee found that these companies collect information ranging from the relatively mundane to the incredibly sensitive, including names and addresses, income levels, and medical histories. They then sell it off without giving serious consideration to what the buyers might do with it.

In the process, you could find yourself categorized as part of a group of "Mid-Life Strugglers: Families" or "Meager Metro Means" or "Oldies but Goodies," which aggregator InfoUSA described as "gullible" people who "want to believe their luck can change." Think of it as high-tech commercial profiling of the most exploitative sort.

Corporate Data Collection Raises Alarms

Kaveh Waddell

Kaveh Waddell is an associate editor at the Atlantic.

D on't be fooled: Congress may have finally passed the bill reining in the National Security Agency's bulk-surveillance programs, but your data is still being collected on the Internet.

Lost in the debate over the NSA is the fact that companies like Google and Facebook continue to vacuum up vast troves of consumer data and use it for marketing.

The private-sector tech companies that run the social networks and email services Americans use every day are relatively opaque when it comes to their data-collection and retention policies, which are engineered not to preserve national security but to bolster the companies' bottom lines.

Critics say the consumer data that private companies collect can paint as detailed a picture of an individual as the metadata that got caught up in the NSA's dragnets. Companies like Google and Facebook comb through customers' usage statistics in order to precisely tailor marketing to their users, a valuable service that advertisers pay the companies dearly to access.

"What both types of information collection show is that metadata—data about data—can in many cases be more revelatory than content," said Gabe Rottman, legislative counsel at the American Civil Liberties Union. "You see that given the granularity with which private data collection can discern very intimate details about your life."

And there's no guarantee what is collected by the private sector will stay with the private sector. "The government has a huge number of tools to get data from private companies," said Chris

Calabrese, senior policy director at the Center for Democracy and Technology. "That's obviously a very difficult situation for companies to be in."

Law-enforcement agencies are looking for even more ways to access private companies' data. Some social-networking sites have begun encrypting the data that's sent through their servers, prompting the FBI to ask companies to make their data available to the agency when asked.

"We suggest, and we are imploring, Congress to help us seek legal remedies towards that as well as asking the companies to provide technological solutions to help that," said Michael Steinbach, assistant director of the FBI's counterterrorism division, at a congressional hearing Wednesday. "Privacy above all other things, including safety and freedom from terrorism, is not where we want to go."

Still, comparing NSA spying and private-sector data-gathering is "a little bit apples to oranges," Calabrese said."There's real concerns around government overreach that have to do with our constitutional values and what we care about as a nation."

Unlike the private sector, Rottman said, "government can take your life or liberty."

When users sign onto Google or Facebook, they choose to give up their personal information in order to get valuable services from the companies, which sets up a dynamic fundamentally different from government surveillance.

But more often than not, Calabrese says, user consent is not enough to justify data collection, because of the lack of transparency in the process. "People aren't always aware of the amount of information being collected about them when they surf online," he said.

"People should be voting with their feet when companies aren't supporting the most aggressive privacy policies," Rottman said. But users are often not informed voters. "You can't vote with your feet unless you know you need to vote with your feet," said Rottman.

Although the Senate's attention has been caught up lately in the debate over government surveillance, legislation introduced earlier this year aimed to bolster data privacy by placing limits on the private sector.

Sen. Ed Markey, D-Mass., is behind two such bills this year. Along with Sen. Orrin Hatch, R-Utah, Markey reintroduced legislation last month that would place security requirements on companies that deal in student data and would forbid them from using student data for advertising.

Markey also reintroduced a more general bill in March aimed at improving the accuracy of personal information stored online. It would require "data brokers"—that is, companies that collect and sell personal data—to have a system by which users can verify that their information is correct and to allow users to choose not to make their data available for marketing.

And Sen. Bernie Sanders, the Democratic presidential candidate, a longtime advocate of data privacy, has turned his trademark ire against both the government's and the private sector's data-collection policies. He calls government surveillance "Orwellian" and presents a bleak picture of agencies obsessed with tracking Americans' every movement, but his criticism is not limited to the government.

"While today we are focusing appropriately on the role of the federal government in issues of civil liberties, we must also understand that it is not just the government that is collecting information on law-abiding Americans," Sanders said in a speech last month. "In fact, the private sector's collection of information is just as intrusive and equally dangerous."

Sanders said during that speech that he will introduce legislation calling for a "comprehensive review of data collection by public and private entities and the impact that that data is having on the American people." That legislation has not yet materialized, and the senator's office remains tight-lipped about the bill.

For their part, various tech companies are paying attention to the trend.

Google on Monday unveiled a frequently asked questions page to address users' privacy concerns, answering questions like "Does Google sell my personal information?" and "How does Google keep my information safe?" It also revamped its account settings page, offering privacy and security "checkups" to walk users through steps to keep their data safe.

On the same day, Facebook announced it will offer the option to send sensitive information, like password reset links, in encrypted emails. ("New Facebook feature shows actual respect for your privacy," read a *Wired* headline on an article about the announcement.) Facebook already encrypts traffic to and from its site, and offers privacy fanatics—or those who fear government retribution for their actions on the social network—access to its services via the Tor browser, widely regarded as the most secure and private way to access the Internet.

The companies' changes are moves in the right direction, according to Calabrese. Although Google's announcement did not include any changes in data collection policy, it did represent an important increase in transparency and accessibility.

"Usability really does matter," Calabrese said. "Too often, privacy controls are hard for consumers to figure out. They tend to get frustrated and not use them."

CHAPTER 4

Does Video Surveillance Make Us Safer?

Overview: Video Surveillance Helps Solve Crime but Jeopardizes Privacy

Michael Jonas

Michael Jonas is executive editor at Commonwealth.

On the day of the Boston Marathon two years ago, before the bombs and the blood, Ed Davis was taking in the race from the viewing stand at the Copley Square finish line. Being a cop as well as a spectator, however, he couldn't help but ponder things cops think about these days, especially if they are the top police official in a city holding a major international sporting event.

"I was sitting in the bleachers that morning watching all the people with cameras," says Davis. "And it occurred to me: If anything happens here, there's going to be a record of it. You can't walk three feet without somebody picking you up in the background of a still shot that they're taking or video they're taking."

Something, of course, did happen. And within 20 minutes of the bomb blasts on that Monday two Aprils ago, says Davis, who was then the city's police commissioner, the order went out to try to locate and secure any photo or video evidence showing the area during the time leading up to the explosions.

Along with canvassing businesses along Boylston Street that may have had surveillance video cameras in operation, officials decided to crowd-source their hunt for leads by asking people to submit any digital photos or video they had from the finish line area. "People were so responsive that it crashed the FBI computers that we had set up to do it," says Davis.

By Wednesday, authorities had images from cameras of nearby businesses showing the two men they believed were responsible for the blasts that killed three people and wounded 260. After

---

an internal debate among local and federal law enforcement officials, the decision was made on Thursday to publicly release the images. Within hours, Tamerlan and Dzhokhar Tsarnaev began what would be the bloody denouement to the region's week of terror, allegedly shooting to death MIT police officer Sean Collier, carjacking a man and his Mercedes SUV, and leading police on a chase to Watertown that ended in a wild shootout that left Tamerlan Tsarnaev dead and his brother, who was found hiding several hours later, badly wounded.

Although the suspects were not identified from the surveillance video, its release is clearly what "activated" them, says Davis. "They realized it would just be a matter of time before they were caught."

The images that were released that week—along with graphic scenes recorded on a camera right in front of one of the blast sites that have not been shared publicly—are sure to figure in Dzhokhar Tsarnaev's trial, which is now playing out in federal court in Boston. The Marathon may be the highest-profile crime in recent years in which video surveillance played a crucial role. But it is by no means the only one.

Hardly a day goes by without a news report of a crime, from the mundane to the murderous, for which there is a surveillance image, with police often seeking public assistance in identifying suspects. It all has the effect of making it seem like technology is helping us get the upper hand on the bad guys, and often it is.

Its role in helping to solve cases after a crime occurs seems evident. Rigorous evidence of video surveillance's crime prevention powers, however, isn't overwhelming, where it exists at all. Meanwhile, civil liberties advocates say the unchecked proliferation of surveillance video, like the potential to poke into our online practices, is yet another way we are being tracked and our privacy is disappearing.

It's a sometimes uneasy balance that we're constantly seeking today, trying to harness the upside of technology without getting overrun by it.

Eyes on London

When it comes to video surveillance of public spaces, England is the undisputed king of cameras. London's "Ring of Steel" surveillance network includes thousands of cameras as well as a license plate reading system that records every vehicle entering the central part of the city. Set up in the late 1990s to combat terrorist bombings by the Irish Republican Army, the surveillance system has grown to include nearly 500,000 cameras in London alone and more than 4 million across the country.

The network of cameras was regarded as crucial to identifying the suicide bombers responsible for four explosions set off on London's transit system in July 2005, and with helping to thwart a planned follow-up attack several weeks later. The bombings killed 52 and injured more than 700.

Davis, the former Boston police commissioner, was doing consulting work in London just after the bombings and met with the head of the city's metropolitan police. "He said unequivocally that if it was not for the cameras they never would have solved that bombing," says Davis. That lesson stayed with Davis. When he found himself in the same shoes eight years later, Davis says he had one immediate thought: "If we're going to solve this Marathon bombing, we've got to concentrate on the video."

While its role in combating major terror attacks was the initial rationale for England's all-in plunge into the world of surveillance video, the 1993 kidnapping of 2-year-old James Bulger, caught on surveillance video at a British shopping mall, may have done more than anything to solidify the country's embrace of cameras on every corner.

Paul Evans, another former Boston police commissioner, got to see the UK fervor for surveillance video up-close. From 2003 to 2007, Evans ran England's Police and Crime Standards Directorate. Whenever he visited a local police department, Evans says, a look at their closed-circuit television monitoring system was invariably the first thing on the tour.

"Every time I'd visit a force, they'd insist that I had to go see their CCTV," he says. "Big Brother was there, and Big Brother was there in a big way," says Evans, citing an estimate that the typical Londoner was captured on video 220 times each day.

"They saw CCTV as a panacea," says Evans, who says he wasn't convinced. "Was it incredibly valuable in solving high-profile crimes? Absolutely. It's probably debatable as to whether it reduced crime."

Brandon Welsh, a Northeastern University criminologist, has carried out what may be the broadest examination of surveillance video and crime prevention. Welsh coauthored a 2009 book, *Making Public Places Safer: Surveillance and Crime Prevention*, that pooled the results from all available, rigorously conducted studies of the question.

"On aggregate, we found that there is a modest, significant effect of cameras in reducing crime," says Welsh. However, much of the overall 16 percent reduction in crime from the combined results of 41 studies came from prevention of vehicle crime in parking lots and garages. There was less evidence of its effect on violent crime.

The book examined several crime-fighting interventions. It turned out that enhanced street lighting "on aggregate was slightly more effective in public places than cameras," says Welsh, with lighting credited with reducing crime by 21 percent.

Welsh and his coauthor, David Farrington of Cambridge University, were commissioned in 2000 by Britain's Home Office to carry out the research. When their initial 2002 report found that something as basic as enhanced street lighting appeared to be more effective in reducing crime than surveillance video, "the British government was not keen to release the studies," says Welsh.

"I have all the clippings from newspapers that were lambasting the British government, because at that point they had spent hundreds of millions of pounds on cameras," he says. The government "had these two criminologists—I'm sure they had other choice words for us—and we were causing a fuss. We wanted to know, what does the evidence say?"

Nancy La Vigne, a researcher at the Urban Institute in Washington, led one of the most detailed examinations of surveillance video in the US in a 2009 study for the Department of Justice. The report examined the use of surveillance cameras in three cities that have made extensive use of the technology: Baltimore, Chicago, and Washington, DC.

In Baltimore, where extensive arrays of cameras were installed in a 50-block downtown area and in three high-crime neighborhoods, property and violent crime appeared to be reduced in the downtown area and in two of the three neighborhoods, with reductions ranging from 8 percent in one neighborhood to 25 percent in the downtown area.

In Chicago, the research found a significant 38 percent crime reduction in one neighborhood targeted with cameras, but little to show for the effort in a second area, though the study notes that the concentration of cameras was much less in the latter. The study of cameras in Washington, DC, did not show any pronounced effects.

So do surveillance cameras prevent crime? "My answer would be a definitive it depends," says La Vigne. "It depends on how they're deployed, it depends on how they're used." She says they have to be in areas where there is a significant crime problem, deployed in great enough numbers to provide a real deterrence, and there have to be resources allotted for monitoring them and following-up incidents picked up on camera.

Police in Fall River think they put together the right ingredients to make a difference. In response to an increase in store robberies in recent years, cameras were installed at 20 small businesses as part of a two-year, $165,000 federal grant. Storeowners were also given tips on other safety measures they could take like clearing things from windows to give an unobstructed view into the store from the street. Police Chief Daniel Racine says the city has seen a 30 percent decrease in robberies of small businesses. "We thought that was pretty significant," he says.

Video Sleuthing

While deploying video surveillance in a way that yields a reduction in crime can be tricky, it is becoming a mainstay of criminal investigations after an incident occurs.

As the Boston Police Department's superintendent of investigative services, Bobby Merner oversees all criminal investigations by the department. The seen-it-all son of Mission Hill has worked the streets in the city's toughest neighborhoods, including time over his 28-year career in the gang unit, the drug unit, and as the head of homicide. Merner knows the human side of how to work a case as well as any cop in the city. But he says surveillance video has become an invaluable aid to those efforts.

"There isn't an incident that happens at any time of any day, any night that the first thing we ask isn't, any cameras?" says Merner. "Because there are so many now. It enhances our investigative abilities greatly."

He says the proliferation of video surveillance, both government and private cameras, has changed the procedures that are followed as soon as officers arrive at a serious crime scene. "One of the first things we do is we conduct something called the canvass," he says. "And the canvass is for witnesses. Who was present at the time? Well, part of the canvass now is to have someone, whether it's a patrol officer or a detective, assigned immediately to check for cameras."

Surveillance cameras have become law enforcement's most reliable witnesses—unflappable observers with photographic memory.

In Boston, the canvass involves determining whether any of the hundreds of city-owned cameras may have had a view of the scene, but it more often means going to area businesses, whose arsenal of private surveillance cameras greatly outnumbers those the city has deployed.

Three Boston detectives who received training from the US Secret Service work under Merner in a special video recovery team that deals with private cameras, while police are also able to download images from the city-operated cameras.

Merner says the department is presently using surveillance video evidence as part of several active murder investigations. "We have some great footage," he says.

Video has played a role in several recent murder cases, including the 2010 conviction of Xzeniyeju Chukwuezi for fatally shooting Solheil Turner in Roxbury in 2007. The early morning shooting of the 15-year-old high school student, who was waiting for a bus to school, shocked the city and seemed all the more chilling because it was captured on surveillance cameras from two nearby stores.

"We're looking for it all the time, and we're getting it in many instances," says Suffolk County district attorney Dan Conley about video evidence.

Surveillance video proved vital in the quick arrest of a suspect in the shooting in November of Chang Ly, a hard-working Vietnamese refugee who was shot while behind the counter of his Dorchester convenience store.

Sometimes cameras provide leads that outfox even more enterprising criminals. In a March 2013 shooting in a Blue Hill Avenue convenience store, the gunman sought to foil any ability to ID him by wearing a mask, but a camera captured the spot where he propped the door to the store open with a bare hand while firing at the clerk with the other. A palm print obtained from that spot on the door proved crucial in making an ID and ultimately securing a guilty plea in the case.

Video can also sometimes make up for reluctant witnesses. "The more we can gain from video surveillance or DNA or those sorts of things, the easier it is for us to solve cases without human beings stepping forward," says Conley.

But there is a flipside to that. As Nancy La Vigne and her colleagues wrote in their Department of Justice report: "Prosecutors cited the 'CSI effect' whereby juries assume that advanced forensic and technological evidence is present at all crime scenes and don't deliver guilty [verdicts] in the absence of camera footage."

Several shootings at or near MBTA stations last fall were quickly followed by arrests aided by surveillance video. "We like to say it's the wave of the future, but the future is here," says Lt. Richard Sullivan of the Transit Police.

Nowhere may the future be more here than across the MBTA's 145 subway stations and its fleet of buses. The T has more than 5,000 cameras deployed throughout its system, giving its facilities by far the most concentrated surveillance-camera presence in the state. The T says it has invested "tens of millions of dollars" in the camera system, almost all of it federal funding, primarily from the Department of Homeland Security.

Sullivan says Transit Police make use of surveillance video "on a daily basis." That includes everything from pursuing leads following violent incidents such as last fall's shootings at T stations to much more low-level offenses that can nonetheless pique public outrage.

Such was the case in November with a video image showing a man pocketing the cellphone of a woman that dropped onto a subway platform as she leapt to her death in front of a Red Line train. By the following day, with the image appearing on television newscasts, news websites, and in newspapers, 26-year-old Josue Gonzalez turned himself—and the phone—in to police.

Jake Wark, a spokesman for Conley, the Suffolk County DA, says surveillance video "plays a part in almost every investigation and prosecution of a crime inside an MBTA bus or station."

While cities like Baltimore and Chicago have set up extensive camera networks in certain areas, Boston has not gone that route apart from the T's extensive camera network. There are 122 cameras operated by police using grant funding from the federal Department of Homeland Security, with another 190 cameras spread across eight immediately surrounding communities. The police department also has several dozen "quick-deploy" cameras that can be set up for special events or easily shifted to areas experiencing crime problems.

Boston also has about 380 cameras along major thoroughfares, designed primarily to aid the city and state transportation departments in traffic monitoring and management, but which can also be viewed from the police information nerve-center in the department's Roxbury headquarters.

Lots of the evidence used to investigate cases, however, comes from private cameras installed by businesses. All of the surveillance video obtained from the Marathon bombing came from private cameras in the area, says Davis.

Boston Police Capt. Richard Sexton says the Dorchester district he's in charge of was hit a couple of years ago by a series of 13 armed robberies of businesses. Once police finally had a video image from one business with a camera and released it publicly, "within a day we had people calling with an identification," says Sexton. He says the perpetrator is now serving a 15-year sentence.

"It definitely has made cases that we wouldn't have had otherwise," Sexton says of the widespread availability of video images.

The Rational Offender

Though there are lots of examples to support Sexton's view, the research world has yet to carry out rigorous studies that provide evidence of a crime-solving effect of surveillance video, says Welsh, the Northeastern University criminologist. The MBTA clearance rates for crimes—the rate at which incidents result in an arrest—are slightly higher than the national average for all police departments, but not by a big margin.

Major crime is down more than 20 percent on the T from levels of a decade ago, but rates have also decreased in Boston as well as nationally over this period.

Sullivan, the Transit Police lieutenant, says he thinks the T's heavy presence of cameras will lead to further reduction beyond any overall decline in crime rates that may occur otherwise. "Eventually, when we have enough time under our belt, I think you will see that this will aid in the overall reduction of crime," he says. "We're hopeful."

The belief that surveillance cameras can have a preventive effect is rooted in a theory of deterrence based on the idea of the "rational offender." "There's this premise that most offenders are acting rationally, there's a weighing of the costs and benefits," says Welsh, the Northeastern criminology professor. "That is good news for all of us—it's not the random spontaneous criminal event that so often makes the front pages. And what that really gets at is the ability to impede or put in place barriers to increase the risks for crime commission," says Welsh.

The T hopes its saturation of stations and buses with cameras is becoming just that barrier. Part of that deterrence effort includes prominently displayed video screens showing passengers on subway platforms or on buses. The hope is that the displays deter "all who may possess nefarious intent while traveling on the MBTA," says Sullivan. He says the T also wants it clear that there is nothing covert about its camera surveillance. "They're not positioned surreptitiously," he says.

The rational offender theory suggests we can appeal to a would-be criminal's sense of reason, and there may be some who think better of their "nefarious intent" once they're aware of the presence of cameras. The population inclined toward crime, however, does not universally think at that higher plane.

"I don't know that they are preventing crime," says Merner, the Boston police superintendent, about video cameras, "because obviously we're still catching a lot of bad guys on video doing a lot of bad things. All you've got to do is watch the evening news to see the latest brain surgeon-criminal doing something on camera."

When police are able to quickly access video surveillance images of a crime, it can help them in looking for fleeing suspects in the immediate area. For investigations after an incident, before releasing an image and seeking public tips, they often share the image within law enforcement circles, looking for leads to a suspect's identify from other officers, probation officials, guards at the South Bay House of Correction, and others who are well-acquainted with the repeat offenders who account for a good portion of those committing crimes.

While that combines technology with old-fashioned street knowledge of offenders among cops and others in law enforcement, the Massachusetts State Police bring the use of surveillance video into the realm of NCIS and other popular culture portrayals of crime fighting using cutting-edge technology. Since 2006, the department has operated a unit that uses facial recognition software to tap the Registry of Motor Vehicles database of drivers' license photographs to aid crime investigations. The specialized unit works with State Police detectives, federal law enforcement, and local police departments to try to match suspect's captured on surveillance video with the RMV database.

In 2013, the unit ran the software program for 441 cases requested by law enforcement agencies and got 123 "hits" that appeared to ID a person in the surveillance image. Through October of last year, the most recent data available from the State Police, the unit had processed 253 requests, with 59 "hits."

Privacy Worries

The use of facial recognition software is just the sort of once-futuristic capability that has arrived, and that makes civil liberties advocates uneasy.

Government has "created, largely in the shadows with zero public debate and very little external oversight, if any, very advanced camera networks that are able to track people throughout the city as they go about their daily lives, and that is a huge problem," says Kade Crockford, director of the technology for liberty program at the American Civil Liberties Union of Massachusetts.

In a series of articles last year, the alternative newsweekly *Dig Boston* reported that Boston engaged in an ambitious snooping exercise during two 2013 concerts held on City Hall Plaza. The paper reported that a city contract with IBM to develop elaborate information systems for municipal government had been extended to include something termed an Intelligent Operations Center.

At the two concerts, the center was used to record video of concertgoers that could then be analyzed using advanced biometric techniques to detect not only facial and body features but also "panic levels and crowd sentiment."

Boston officials say the exercise was a pilot program that has not been continued.

"Under the previous administration, the city of Boston engaged in a pilot program with IBM, testing situational awareness software," Kate Norton, a spokeswoman for Mayor Marty Walsh, said in a statement. She said the city did not see "practical value" in the system and "did not pursue a long-term use of this software or enter into a contract to utilize this software on a permanent basis." She added, however, that as the city "explores new technology and new public safety tools, it may not necessarily be practical or appropriate to disclose every test or demonstration."

As for the State Police facial recognition software unit, officials say it is used only in pursuing crime leads. "We do not use facial recognition software to identify images of persons recorded outside of an ongoing investigation into a specific crime," spokesman David Procopio said in a statement. "For instance, we would not use it to identify random images of people photographed in a crowd or a demonstration."

While police departments hear from those concerned about privacy issues and the potential for video surveillance to be used to gather information on law-abiding citizens, they also hear from those eager to see cameras installed in the hope that they will bring some added measure of safety to an area.

In Worcester, the City Council voted in December to install 20 to 30 cameras in two neighborhoods experiencing crime problems. They will be tied in to the city's police headquarters. Some residents appeared at a December hearing and raised concerns about the cameras, but none of them were from the neighborhoods where they are to be installed, says Ed Augustus, the Worcester city manager. People in the affected neighborhoods, who said, "'Hey, I don't feel safe on the streets and worry about my kids walking here'—they were interested in the cameras," says Augustus.

Last year, Boston Mayor Marty Walsh established an initiative to allow young people aged 12 to 25 to weigh in on how to spend $1 million out of the city's capital budget. More than 1,500 people cast ballots in the process. One of the projects selected was the installation of surveillance cameras at Dr. Loesch Family Park in Dorchester, a park with a tortured history of problems, including violent encounters, that residents are committed to turning around.

"In the end, people up there wanted them," says Sexton, the local police commander, about the cameras being installed.

Emmett Folgert has spent more than three decades working with young people in Dorchester, trying to steer them away from trouble and pull those who have already found their way to it back toward more productive pursuits.

Folgert, director of the Dorchester Youth Collaborative, thinks the presence of surveillance cameras is, on balance, a helpful development, pointing out that it's urban youth who are most often the ones who are victims of violence. "They're really scared, and with the cameras, that gives them some safety," he says. "So many people who are commenting on this don't live in these neighborhoods and they are not young. They don't understand the terror that happens in unsupervised spaces when you have organized gangs."

The newest wrinkle in the debate over surveillance video is the rising call for police officers to wear body cameras that capture their activity and interactions with the public. The demands for body cameras have come in the wake of the deaths at the hands of police of unarmed black men in Ferguson, Missouri, and Staten Island, New York. President Obama announced in early December that he was requesting $75 million in funding for 50,000 police body cameras.

The evidence, to date, on their impact is limited, but bodycams are likely here to stay. "I think that clearly is going to be a trend here in the United States," says Davis, who thinks the wearable tiny cameras are, on balance, a plus. "It improves the conduct of the police. It also improves the conduct of the people interacting with the police," he says. "I think it helps both sides."

Mayor Walsh reacted coolly to the idea. "My answer was I think the problem goes a lot deeper than body cameras," says Walsh. "A camera's not going to build a relationship between a police officer and young person on the street. That's still my answer, but we will still be open to body cameras in pilot programs."

Segun Idowu, cofounder of a Boston group pushing for police body cameras that formed following the Ferguson shooting, says he and the roughly 50 members of the Boston Police Camera Action Team are determined to drive concrete change. "We were tired of just sitting around and complaining," says Idowu, a 26-year-old Morehouse College graduate. "We've been having conversations on race. All we ever do when things happen is we talk."

Many have pointed to the Eric Garner case in New York as evidence of the limits to what body cameras might achieve. Garner died after being put in a chokehold by a New York police officer, an episode that was captured on a bystander's cellphone, but a grand jury voted not to bring any charges.

"All of us were very let down at the decision, given that there was video evidence," says Idowu. "We don't have all the answers. But I am not ready to concede the notion that body cameras are not going to work simply because of this one high-profile case."

For his part, Merner, the Boston police superintendent, takes a cautious approach to the technology. "Look, I think it's something that should be explored," says Merner. "But I think folks think this is a be-all, end-all."

There are all sorts of details to be worked out around the use of body cameras—when are they on, how long is information stored. Merner is quick to highlight ways that the use of body cameras could set things back. "I've been doing this for ages—drugs, gangs, homicide," he says, ticking off the various units he's worked and sometimes directed, developing contacts and trust in city neighborhoods. "People talk to me all the time. 'Hey, Bobby, you might want to take a look down the street. There's a blue van. Or shoot up by Orchard Park.' Those days will be gone if you have a bodycam on."

Maintaining Balance

The fact that some of the same civil liberties advocates pushing for wider use of police body cameras are also raising questions about the proliferation of surveillance cameras under the guise of crime prevention or control underscores a dimension to the issue that is often overlooked in discussing this or any other new technology.

"It's a tool like any other tool," says Gary Marx, emeritus professor of sociology at MIT who has written extensively about surveillance. "It's not inherently good or bad." Marx says it's "important not to get swept off one's cultural or ideological feet by the various claims" about video surveillance, whether they are touting its wonders or sounding the alarm over the dangers it poses. "The key is a little humility and skepticism," he says.

The discussion, at this point, is hardly one centered only on government and how far it goes in watching us.

"We've definitely given up a bit of our privacy, but it's not so much due to government. It's more due to technology," says Davis. "The cat is out of the bag. Whether the city of Boston decides to buy a thousand cameras tomorrow or they don't makes no difference, because there's 10,000 cameras out there in the private sector."

Surveillance video is surely not a magic bullet that will eradicate crime, let alone eliminate the social factors that are often behind it. But it may, when well-publicized and heavily deployed, help to reset norms in places like transit systems. And it's hard to argue that it's not valuable in investigating and solving crime given the steady stream of cases in which video evidence appears to help crack a case or strengthen it.

The question we'll have to grapple with is whether there's a point at which we have too much of a good thing.

"There is a level of intrusion of video into our lives that, as a society, we've yet to figure out where the limits are and where they should be," says Jerry Ratcliffe, director of the Center for Security and Crime Science at Temple University in Philadelphia. "Civil liberties groups, on the other hand, tend to be concerned about civil rights and ignore the ability to reduce or solve crime. We need a mature conversation as a society. There's a great deal of benefit potentially from these systems, but nothing's for free."

Even Davis, offering an example that is a little surprising coming from Boston's former top cop, is a bit wistful about how much technology has changed things. "I have a little nostalgia for the old days, when if you were a teenager you might be able to drink a beer without somebody watching you do it," he says. "But I think that the cost-benefit analysis weighs heavily that this is a good thing."

Potential Benefits of the Coming Surveillance State

Stuart Armstrong

Stuart Armstrong is a research fellow at the Future of Humanity Institute in Oxford, where he works on decision theory and the risks of artificial intelligence.

Suppose you're walking home one night, alone, and you decide to take a shortcut through a dark alley. You make it halfway through, when suddenly you hear some drunks stumbling behind you. Some of them are shouting curses. They look large and powerful, and there are several of them. Nonetheless, you feel safe, because you know someone is watching.

You know this because you live in the future where surveillance is universal, ubiquitous and unavoidable. Governments and large corporations have spread cameras, microphones and other tracking devices all across the globe, and they also have the capacity to store and process oceans of surveillance data in real time. Big Brother not only watches your sex life, he analyses it. It sounds nightmarish—but it might be inevitable. So far, attempts to control surveillance have generally failed. We could be headed straight for the panopticon, and if recent news developments are any indication, it might not take that long to get there.

Maybe we should start preparing. And not just by wringing our hands or mounting attempts to defeat surveillance. For if there's a chance that the panopticon is inevitable, we ought to do some hard thinking about its positive aspects. Cataloguing the downsides of mass surveillance is important, essential even. But we have a whole literature devoted to that. Instead, let's explore its potential benefits.

"Life in the Fishbowl," Stuart Armstrong, Aeon Media Group, September 30, 2013. Reprinted with permission of Stuart Armstrong, University of Oxford.

The first, and most obvious, advantage of mass surveillance is a drastic reduction in crime. Indeed, this is the advantage most often put forward by surveillance proponents today. The evidence as to whether current surveillance achieves this is ambiguous; cameras, for instance, seem to have an effect on property crime, but not on incidences of violence. But today's world is very different from a panopticon full of automatically analysed surveillance devices that leave few zones of darkness.

If calibrated properly, total surveillance might eradicate certain types of crime almost entirely. People respond well to inevitable consequences, especially those that follow swiftly on the heels of their conduct. Few would commit easily monitored crimes such as assault or breaking and entering, if it meant being handcuffed within minutes. This kind of ultra-efficient police capability would require not only sensors capable of recording crimes, but also advanced computer vision and recognition algorithms capable of detecting crimes quickly. There has been some recent progress on such algorithms, with further improvements expected. In theory, they would be able to alert the police in real time, while the crime was still ongoing. Prompt police responses would create near-perfect deterrence, and violent crime would be reduced to a few remaining incidents of overwhelming passion or extreme irrationality.

If surveillance recordings were stored for later analysis, other types of crimes could be eradicated as well, because perpetrators would fear later discovery and punishment. We could expect crimes such as low-level corruption to vanish, because bribes would become perilous (to demand or receive) for those who are constantly under watch. We would likely see a similar reduction in police brutality. There might be an initial spike in detected cases of police brutality under a total surveillance regime, as incidents that would previously have gone unnoticed came to light, but then, after a short while, the numbers would tumble. Ubiquitous video recording, mobile and otherwise, has already begun to expose such incidents.

On a smaller scale, mass surveillance would combat all kinds of abuses that currently go unreported because the abuser has power over the abused. You see this dynamic in a variety of scenarios, from the dramatic (child abuse) to the more mundane (line managers insisting on illegal, unpaid overtime). Even if the victim is too scared to report the crime, the simple fact that the recordings existed would go a long way towards equalising existing power differentials. There would be the constant risk of some auditor or analyst stumbling on the recording, and once the abused was out of the abuser's control (grown up, in another job) they could retaliate and complain, proof in hand. The possibility of deferred vengeance would make abuse much less likely to occur in the first place.

With reduced crime, we could also expect a significant reduction in police work and, by extension, police numbers. Beyond a rapid-reaction force tasked with responding to rare crimes of passion, there would be no need to keep a large police force on hand. And there would also be no need for them to enjoy the special rights they do today. Police officers can, on mere suspicion, detain you, search your person, interrogate you, and sometimes enter your home. They can also arrest you on suspicion of vague "crimes" such as "loitering with intent." Our present police force is given these powers because it needs to be able to investigate. Police officers can't be expected to know who committed what crime, and when, so they need extra powers to be able to figure this out, and still more special powers to protect themselves while they do so. But in a total-surveillance world, there would be no need for humans to have such extensive powers of investigation. For most crimes, guilt or innocence would be obvious and easy to establish from the recordings. The police's role could be reduced to arresting specific individuals, who have violated specific laws.

If all goes well, there might be fewer laws for the police to enforce. Most countries currently have an excess of laws, criminalising all sorts of behaviour. This is only tolerated because of selective enforcement; the laws are enforced very rarely, or only against marginalised groups. But if everyone was suddenly subject to enforcement, there would have to be a mass legal repeal. When spliffs on private yachts are punished as severely as spliffs in the ghetto, you can expect the marijuana legalisation movement to gather steam. When it becomes glaringly obvious that most people simply can't follow all the rules they're supposed to, these rules will have to be reformed. In the end, there is a chance that mass surveillance could result in more personal freedom, not less.

The military is another arm of state power that is ripe for a surveillance-inspired shrinking. If cross-border surveillance becomes ubiquitous and effective, we could see a reduction in the $1.7 trillion that the world spends on the military each year. Previous attempts to reduce armaments have ultimately been stymied by a lack of reliable verification. Countries can never trust that their enemies aren't cheating, and that encourages them to cheat themselves. Arms races are also made worse by a psychological phenomenon, whereby each side interprets the actions of the other as a dangerous provocation, while interpreting its own as purely defensive or reactive. With cross-border mass surveillance, countries could check that others are abiding by the rules, and that they weren't covertly preparing for an attack. If intelligence agencies were to use all the new data to become more sophisticated observers, countries might develop a better understanding of each other. Not in the hand-holding, peace-and-love sense, but in knowing what is a genuine threat and what is bluster or posturing. Freed from fear of surprising new weapons, and surprise attacks, countries could safely shrink their militaries. And with reduced armies, we should be able to expect reduced warfare, continuing the historical trend in conflict reduction since the end of the Second World War.

Of course, these considerations pale when compared with the potential for mass surveillance to help prevent global catastrophic risks, and other huge disasters. Pandemics, to name just one example, are among the deadliest dangers facing the human race. The Black Death killed a third of Europe's population in the 14th century and, in the early 20th century, the Spanish Flu killed off between 50 and 100 million people. In addition, smallpox buried more people than the two world wars combined. There is no reason to think that great pandemics are a thing of the past, and in fact there are reasons to think that another plague could be due soon. There is also the possibility that a pandemic could arise from synthetic biology, the human manipulation of microbes to perform specific tasks. Experts are divided as to the risks involved in this new technology, but they could be tremendous, especially if someone were to release, accidentally or malevolently, infectious agents deliberately engineered for high transmissibility and deadliness.

Mass surveillance could help greatly here, by catching lethal pandemics in their earliest stages, or beforehand, if we were to see one being created artificially. It could also expose lax safety standards or dangerous practices in legitimate organisations. Surveillance could allow for quicker quarantines, and more effective treatment of pandemics. Medicines and doctors could be rushed to exactly the right places, and micro quarantines could be instituted. More dramatic measures, such as airport closures, are hard to implement on a large scale, but these quick-response tactics could be implemented narrowly and selectively. Most importantly, those infected could be rapidly informed of their condition, allowing them to seek prompt treatment.

With proper procedures and perfect surveillance, we could avoid pandemics altogether. Infections would be quickly isolated and eliminated, and eradication campaigns would be shockingly efficient. Tracking the movements and actions of those who fell ill would make it much easier to research the causes and pathology of diseases. You can imagine how many lives would have been saved had AIDS been sniffed out by epidemiologists more swiftly.

Likewise, mass surveillance could prevent the terrorist use of nukes, dirty bombs, or other futuristic weapons. Instead of blanket bans in dangerous research areas, we could allow research to proceed and use surveillance to catch bad actors and bad practices. We might even see an increase in academic freedom.

Surveillance could also be useful in smaller, more conventional disasters. Knowing where everyone in a city was at the moment an earthquake struck would make rescue services much more effective, and the more cameras around when hurricanes hit, the better. Over time, all of this footage would increase our understanding of disasters, and help us to mitigate their effects.

Indeed, there are whole new bodies of research that could emerge from the data provided by mass surveillance. Instead of formulating theories and laboriously recruiting a biased and sometimes unwilling group for testing, social scientists, economists and epidemiologists could use surveillance data to test their ideas. And they could do it from home, immediately, and have access to the world's entire population. Many theories could be rapidly confirmed or discarded, with great benefit to society. The panopticon would be a research nirvana.

Mass surveillance could also make our lives more convenient, by eliminating the need for passwords. The surveillance system itself could be used for identification, provided the algorithms were sufficiently effective. Instead of Mr John Smith typing in 'passw0rd!!!' to access his computer or "2345" to access his money, the system could simply track where he was at all times, and grant him access to any computers and money he had the right to. Long security lines at airports could also be eliminated. If surveillance can detect prohibited items, then searches are a waste of time. Effective crime detection and deterrence would mean that people would have little reason to lock their cars or their doors.

Doing business in a mass surveillance society would be smoother, too. Outdoor festivals and concerts would no longer need high fences, security patrols, and intimidating warnings. They could simply replace them with clear signs along the boundary of the event, as anyone attending would be identified and billed directly. People could dash into a shop, grab what they needed, and run out, without having to wait in line or check out. The camera system would have already billed them. Drivers who crashed into parked cars would no longer need to leave a note. They'd be tracked anyway, and insurance companies would have already settled the matter by the time they returned home. Everyday human interactions would be changed in far-reaching ways. Lying and hypocrisy would become practically impossible, and one could no longer project a false image of oneself. In the realm of personal identity, there would be less place for imagination or reinvention, and more place for honesty.

Today's intricate copyright laws could be simplified, and there would be no need for the infantilising mess of reduced functionality that is "Digital Rights Management." Surveillance would render DRM completely unnecessary, meaning that anyone who purchased a song could play it anytime, on any machine, while copying it and reusing it to their heart's content. There would be no point in restricting these uses, because the behaviour that copyrights holders object to—passing the music on to others—would be detected and tagged separately. Every time you bought a song, a book, or even a movie, you'd do so knowing that it would be with you wherever you went for the rest of your life.

The virtues and vices of surveillance are the imagined virtues and vices of small villages, which tend to be safe and neighbourly, but prejudiced and judgemental. With the whole world as the village, we can hope that the multiplicity of cultures and lifestyles would reduce a global surveillance culture's built-in potential for prejudice and judgment. With people more trusting, and less fearful, of each other, we could become more willing to help out, more willing to take part in common projects, more pro-social and more considerate. Yes, these potential benefits aren't the whole story on mass surveillance, and I would never argue that they outweigh the potential downsides. But if we're headed into a future panopticon, we'd better brush up on the possible upsides. Because governments might not bestow these benefits willingly—we will have to make sure to demand them.

Surveillance Keeps Us Safe, Even From the Police

Russell Dean Covey

Russell Dean Covey is a professor of law at Georgia State University. His research is focused on criminal law and procedure.

Michael Brown's recent shooting death by Ferguson police officer Darren Wilson illustrates the pressing importance of digitally documenting police activity, while Eric Garner's case illustrates the limits. Had Officer Wilson been wearing a body camera, we would have a far better understanding of just what, exactly, triggered Brown's death. But the existence of a video capturing Garner's death-by-chokehold was not enough to persuade a New York grand jury to indict. So what does this tell us about the value of recordings?

We need recordings, and we need them not just to investigate high-profile shootings. There is a growing demand for accurate recording of the entire spectrum of police activity, making greater transparency of policing an urgent priority. However, recordings by themselves are not a magic bullet.

The need for more recording is undeniable. Unless a bystander has a cell-phone camera ready, our knowledge of contested facts too often depends solely on the reports of police officers and the citizens with whom they interact. Although we know that most police officers do make a good faith effort to accurately report the facts, we also know that some officers do not. For instance, according to a recent survey one out of every seventeen Denver police officers has been subject to administrative discipline for "departing from the truth" in matters related to their official duties That figure counts only those who have been formally sanctioned. Concerns about police dishonesty extend throughout the evidence-gathering phases of criminal procedure. Police officers have been found lying about observing suspects engaged in illegal activities, where and how contraband was recovered, and whether suspects consented to searches, were given Miranda warnings, or confessed.

The mind can play tricks on us

Even when police make good faith efforts to comply with the law, unintentional bias, poor memory, and sloppy procedures can undermine the accuracy of arrest reports, interview reports, and testimony. This leads investigators and courts to make incorrect inferences regarding the reliability or admissibility of evidence or even, in some cases, about a defendant's substantive guilt.

Problems of this sort arise because the investigatory process occurs in a black box. Absent blind trust in the accuracy and honesty of first person accounts, we cannot be confident that we know what really happened.

While there are limits, digital recording technology presents a promising solution. Although some jurisdictions have begun to experiment with new recording technology, no jurisdiction has implemented a comprehensive digital recording requirement for all police activities. But it could be done. The technology now exists to cheaply and easily document all aspects of a police investigation.

Stationhouse questioning and lineup administration could be easily handled through use of conventional video recording devices. Dashboard cameras already record highway stops in numerous jurisdictions. For encounters in the field, as President Obama recent urged, so-called "body worn video" could cheaply and easily be used to document police-citizen encounters.

There are numerous reasons to use technology to monitor police activity. Visual recordings provide far more complete and accurate evidence of key evidentiary events, such as police-citizen confrontations, confessions and eyewitness identifications. Without recording, prosecutors, defense lawyers, judges, and juries are all left reconstructing the key events of an investigation based on often conflicting hearsay accounts from police, the defendant, and eyewitnesses. Given the ease of making a digital recordings, it is simply crazy to expect juries routinely to accept police officers' hearsay accounts when they could instead be presented a real-time recording of the event.

Given the obvious advantages, the question is not whether we should routinely record police activity, but why such recording technology hasn't already been more widely adopted.

Police have their own reasons for objecting to video

There are four main reasons. First, police departments believe, rightly or wrongly, that secrecy is vital to their effectiveness, and that courts and the general public will misperceive or misinterpret their conduct if they are caught taking shortcuts. Second, even entirely by-the-book police officers resist pervasive recording because of privacy concerns. Third, figuring out how to handle massive amounts of digital data presents real hurdles, and courts are reluctant to devote the resources needed to sift through the massive amounts of data that would be produced by pervasive recording, nor have they mastered how such data can be presented to jurors cheaply, efficiently, and consistent with traditional rules of evidence. Finally, police departments point to tight budgets as a reason not to invest in digital recording.

While these are real concerns, they are not insurmountable. Jurors are surprisingly sophisticated when it comes to understanding, and tolerating, legitimate but deceptive or devious investigative strategies. The police need for tactical secrecy must, at some point, give way to the need to deter police misconduct and document facts that might be critical to the determination of guilt and innocence.

Likewise, police officers' potential privacy concerns, while understandable, are overstated. Employers generally are free to surveil their employees as long as they provide adequate notice. Police officers, moreover, are uniquely public actors and are routinely expected to perform their duties in front of spectators.

(Of course, privacy concerns are not limited to police, and may be even more acutely felt by citizens who interact with them. Protections would need to be developed for them.) Finally, neither court procedures nor police budgets should stand in the way. The expense of digital cameras is relatively small. If using cameras prevents even one one major civil rights lawsuit, it would more than cover the costs. And whether or not we move toward widespread recording, big data is coming, and lawyers and courts will have to learn to handle it. The justice system will adapt.

Of course, cameras are no panacea. The Eric Garner case is only the latest reminder that people can see an event for themselves and still disagree about what happened. The difference, however, is that with the video, we have a basis for discussion. Like the Rodney King beating before it, the recording is the prerequisite for the conversation that followed. Factual knowledge is needed to figure out how, or whether, things must change. And increased transparency is needed not just in force cases, but at every stage of criminal justice. As both the Michael Brown and Eric Garner cases so tragically demonstrate, we need to know the facts. That much is obvious. Figuring out what to do with that knowledge is more difficult, and even more essential.

Too Much Surveillance is Contrary to Human Rights

Angela Watercutter

Angela Watercutter is a senior associate editor at WIRED, *covering entertainment and pop culture.*

Editor's Note: Given Richard Stallman's longtime role in promoting software that respects user freedom (including GNU, which just turned 30), his suggested "remedies" for all the ways technology can be re-designed to provide benefits while avoiding surveillance—like the smart meters example he shares below—seem particularly relevant.

The current level of general surveillance in society is incompatible with human rights. To recover our freedom and restore democracy, we must reduce surveillance to the point where it is possible for whistleblowers of all kinds to talk with journalists without being spotted. To do this reliably, we must reduce the surveillance capacity of the systems we use.

Using free/libre software, as I've advocated for 30 years, is the first step in taking control of our digital lives. We can't trust non-free software; the NSA uses and even creates security weaknesses in non-free software so as to invade our own computers and routers. Free software gives us control of our own computers, but that won't protect our privacy once we set foot on the internet.

Bipartisan legislation to "curtail the domestic surveillance powers" in the U.S. is being drawn up, but it relies on limiting the government's use of our virtual dossiers. That won't suffice to protect whistleblowers if "catching the whistleblower" is grounds for access sufficient to identify him or her. We need to go further.

"Stallman: How Much Surveillance Can Democracy Withstand?" Angela Watercutter, *Wired*, October 14, 2013. Reprinted by permission.

Thanks to Edward Snowden's disclosures, we know that the current level of general surveillance in society is incompatible with human rights. The repeated harassment and prosecution of dissidents, sources, and journalists provides confirmation. We need to reduce the level of general surveillance, but how far? Where exactly is the *maximum tolerable level of surveillance*, beyond which it becomes oppressive? That happens when surveillance interferes with the functioning of democracy: when whistleblowers (such as Snowden) are likely to be caught.

Don't Agree We Need to Reduce Surveillance? Then Read This Section First

If whistleblowers don't dare reveal crimes and lies, we lose the last shred of effective control over our government and institutions. That's why surveillance that enables the state to find out who has talked with a reporter is too much surveillance—too much for democracy to endure. An unnamed U.S. government official ominously told journalists in 2011 that the U.S. would not subpoena reporters because "We know who you're talking to." Sometimes journalists' phone call records are subpoenaed to find this out, but Snowden has shown us that in effect they subpoena all the phone call records of everyone in the U.S., all the time.

Opposition and dissident activities need to keep secrets from states that are willing to play dirty tricks on them. The ACLU has demonstrated the U.S. government's systematic practice of infiltrating peaceful dissident groups on the pretext that there might be terrorists among them. The point at which surveillance is too much is the point at which the state can find who spoke to a known journalist or a known dissident.

Information, Once Collected, Will Be Misused

When people recognize that the level of general surveillance is too high, the first response is to propose limits on access to the accumulated data. That sounds nice, but it won't fix the problem, not even slightly, even supposing that the government obeys the rules. (The NSA has misled the FISA court, which said it was unable to effectively hold the NSA accountable.) Suspicion of a crime will be grounds for access, so once a whistleblower is accused of "espionage," finding the "spy" will provide an excuse to access the accumulated material.

The state's surveillance staff will misuse the data for personal reasons too. Some NSA agents used U.S. surveillance systems to track their lovers—past, present, or wished-for—in a practice called "LoveINT." The NSA says it has caught and punished this a few times; we don't know how many other times it wasn't caught. But these events shouldn't surprise us, because police have long used their access to driver's license records to track down someone attractive, a practice known as "running a plate for a date."

Surveillance data will always be used for other purposes, even if this is prohibited. Once the data has been accumulated and the state has the possibility of access to it, it may misuse that data in dreadful ways.

Total surveillance plus vague law provides an opening for a massive fishing expedition against any desired target. To make journalism and democracy safe, we must limit the accumulation of data that is easily accessible to the state.

Robust Protection for Privacy Must Be Technical

The Electronic Frontier Foundation and other organizations propose a set of legal principles designed to prevent the abuses of massive surveillance. These principles include, crucially, explicit legal protection for whistleblowers; as a consequence, they would be adequate for protecting democratic freedoms—if adopted completely and enforced without exception forever.

However, such legal protections are precarious: as recent history shows, they can be repealed (as in the FISA Amendments Act), suspended, or ignored.

Meanwhile, demagogues will cite the usual excuses as grounds for total surveillance; any terrorist attack, even one that kills just a handful of people, will give them an opportunity.

If limits on access to the data are set aside, it will be as if they had never existed: years worth of dossiers would suddenly become available for misuse by the state and its agents and, if collected by companies, for their private misuse as well. If, however, we stop the collection of dossiers on everyone, those dossiers won't exist, and there will be no way to compile them retroactively. A new illiberal regime would have to implement surveillance afresh, and it would only collect data starting at that date. As for suspending or momentarily ignoring this law, the idea would hardly make sense.

We Must Design Every System for Privacy

If we don't want a total surveillance society, we must consider surveillance a kind of social pollution, and limit the surveillance impact of each new digital system just as we limit the environmental impact of physical construction.

For example: "Smart" meters for electricity are touted for sending the power company moment-by-moment data about each customer's electric usage, including how usage compares with users in general. This is implemented based on general surveillance, but does not require any surveillance. It would be easy for the power company to calculate the average usage in a residential neighborhood by dividing the total usage by the number of subscribers, and send that to the meters. Each customer's meter could compare her usage, over any desired period of time, with the average usage pattern for that period. The same benefit, with no surveillance!

We need to design such privacy into all our digital systems.

Remedy for Collecting Data: Leaving It Dispersed

One way to make monitoring safe for privacy is to keep the data dispersed and inconvenient to access. Old-fashioned security cameras were no threat to privacy. The recording was stored on the premises, and kept for a few weeks at most. Because of the inconvenience of accessing these recordings, it was never done massively; they were accessed only in the places where someone reported a crime. It would not be feasible to physically collect millions of tapes every day and watch them or copy them.

Nowadays, security cameras have become surveillance cameras: they are connected to the internet so recordings can be collected in a data center and saved forever. This is already dangerous, but it is going to get worse. Advances in face recognition may bring the day when suspected journalists can be tracked on the street all the time to see who they talk with.

Internet-connected cameras often have lousy digital security themselves, so anyone could watch what the camera sees. To restore privacy, we should ban the use of internet-connected cameras aimed where and when the public is admitted, except when carried by people. Everyone must be free to post photos and video recordings occasionally, but the systematic accumulation of such data on the internet must be limited.

Remedy for Internet Commerce Surveillance

Most data collection comes from people's own digital activities. Usually the data is collected first by companies. But when it comes to the threat to privacy and democracy, it makes no difference whether surveillance is done directly by the state or farmed out to a business, because the data that the companies collect is systematically available to the state.

The NSA, through PRISM, has gotten into the databases of many large internet corporations. AT&T has saved all its phone call records since 1987 and makes them available to the DEA to search on request. Strictly speaking, the U.S. government does not possess that data, but in practical terms it may as well possess it.

The goal of making journalism and democracy safe therefore requires that we reduce the data collected about people by any organization, not just by the state. We must redesign digital systems so that they do not accumulate data about their users. If they need digital data about our transactions, they should not be allowed to keep them more than a short time beyond what is inherently necessary for their dealings with us.

One of the motives for the current level of surveillance of the internet is that sites are financed through advertising based on tracking users' activities and propensities. This converts a mere annoyance—advertising that we can learn to ignore—into a surveillance system that harms us whether we know it or not. Purchases over the internet also track their users. And we are all aware that "privacy policies" are more excuses to violate privacy than commitments to uphold it.

We could correct both problems by adopting a system of anonymous payments—anonymous for the payer, that is. (We don't want the payee to dodge taxes.) Bitcoin is not anonymous, but technology for digital cash was first developed 25 years ago; we need only suitable business arrangements, and for the state not to obstruct them.

A further threat from sites' collection of personal data is that security breakers might get in, take it, and misuse it. This includes customers' credit card details. An anonymous payment system would end this danger: a security hole in the site can't hurt you if the site knows nothing about you.

Remedy for Travel Surveillance

We must convert digital toll collection to anonymous payment (using digital cash, for instance). License-plate recognition systems recognize all license plates, and the data can be kept indefinitely; they should be required by law to notice and record only those license numbers that are on a list of cars sought by court orders. A less secure alternative would record all cars locally but only for a few days, and not make the full data available over the internet; access to the data should be limited to searching for a list of court-ordered license-numbers.

The U.S. "no-fly" list must be abolished because it is punishment without trial.

It is acceptable to have a list of people whose person and luggage will be searched with extra care, and anonymous passengers on domestic flights could be treated as if they were on this list. It is also acceptable to bar non-citizens, if they are not permitted to enter the country at all, from boarding flights to the country. This ought to be enough for all legitimate purposes.

Many mass transit systems use some kind of smart cards or RFIDs for payment. These systems accumulate personal data: if you once make the mistake of paying with anything but cash, they associate the card permanently with your name. Furthermore, they record all travel associated with each card. Together they amount to massive surveillance. This data collection must be reduced.

Navigation services do surveillance: the user's computer tells the map service the user's location and where the user wants to go; then the server determines the route and sends it back to the user's computer, which displays it. Nowadays, the server probably records the user's locations, since there is nothing to prevent it. This surveillance is not inherently necessary, and redesign could avoid it: free/libre software in the user's computer could download map data for the pertinent regions (if not downloaded previously), compute the route, and display it, without ever telling anyone where the user is or wants to go.

Systems for borrowing bicycles, etc., can be designed so that the borrower's identity is known only inside the station where the item was borrowed. Borrowing would inform all stations that the item is "out", so when the user returns it at any station (in general, a different one), that station will know where and when that item was borrowed. It will inform the other station that the item is no longer "out." It will also calculate the user's bill, and send it (after waiting some random number of minutes) to headquarters along a ring of stations, so that headquarters would not find out which station the bill came from. Once this is done, the return station would forget all about the transaction. If an item remains "out" for too long, the station where it was borrowed can inform headquarters; in that case, it could send the borrower's identity immediately.

Remedy for Communications Dossiers

Internet service providers and telephone companies keep extensive data on their users' contacts (browsing, phone calls, etc). With mobile phones, they also record the user's physical location. They keep these dossiers for a long time: over 30 years, in the case of AT&T. Soon they will even record the user's body activities. It appears that the NSA collects cell phone location data in bulk.

Unmonitored communication is impossible where systems create such dossiers. So it should be illegal to create or keep them. ISPs and phone companies must not be allowed to keep this information for very long, in the absence of a court order to surveil a certain party.

This solution is not entirely satisfactory, because it won't physically stop the government from collecting all the information immediately as it is generated—which is what the U.S. does with some or all phone companies. We would have to rely on prohibiting that by law. However, that would be better than the current situation, where the relevant law (the PATRIOT Act) does not clearly prohibit the practice. In addition, if the government did resume this sort of surveillance, it would not get data about everyone's phone calls made prior to that time.

But Some Surveillance Is Necessary

For the state to find criminals, it needs to be able to investigate specific crimes, or specific suspected planned crimes, under a court order. With the internet, the power to tap phone conversations would naturally extend to the power to tap internet connections. This power is easy to abuse for political reasons, but it is also necessary. Fortunately, this won't make it possible to find whistleblowers after the fact.

Individuals with special state-granted power, such as police, forfeit their right to privacy and must be monitored. (In fact, police have their own jargon term for perjury, "testilying," since they do it so frequently, particularly about protesters and photographers.) One city in California that required police to wear video cameras all the time found their use of force fell by 60%. The ACLU is in favor of this.

Corporations are not people, and not entitled to human rights. It is legitimate to require businesses to publish the details of processes that might cause chemical, biological, nuclear, fiscal, computational (e.g., DRM) or political (e.g., lobbying) hazards to society, to whatever level is needed for public well-being. The danger of these operations (consider the BP oil spill, the Fukushima meltdowns, and the 2008 fiscal crisis) dwarfs that of terrorism.

However, journalism must be protected from surveillance even when it is carried out as part of a business.

Digital technology has brought about a tremendous increase in the level of surveillance of our' movements, actions, and communications. It is far more than we experienced in the 1990s, and far more than people behind the Iron Curtain experienced in the 1980s, and would still be far more even with additional legal limits on state use of the accumulated data.

Unless we believe that our free countries previously suffered from a grave surveillance deficit, and ought to be surveilled more than the Soviet Union and East Germany were, we must reverse this increase. That requires stopping the accumulation of big data about people.

Surveillance Inhibits Moral Decision Making

Emrys Westacott

Emrys Westacott is professor of philosophy at Alfred University in Alfred, New York. This article first appeared in Philosophy Now, *Issue 79, 2010.*

I magine that right after briefing Adam about which fruit was allowed and which forbidden, God had installed a closed-circuit television camera in the garden of Eden, trained on the tree of knowledge. Think how this might have changed things for the better. The serpent sidles up to Eve and urges her to try the forbidden fruit. Eve reaches her hand out—in paradise the fruit is always conveniently within reach—but at the last second she notices the CCTV and thinks better of it. Result: no sin, no Fall, no expulsion from paradise. We don't have to toil among thorns and thistles for the rest of our lives, earning our bread by the sweat of our brows; childbirth is painless; and we feel no need to wear clothes.

So why didn't God do that and save everyone a lot of grief? True, surveillance technology was in its infancy back then, but He could have managed it, and it wouldn't have undermined Eve's free will. She still has a choice to make; but once she sees the camera she's more likely to make the right choice. The most likely explanation would be that God doesn't just want Adam and Eve to make the right choices; he wants them to make the right choices *for the right reasons*. Not eating the forbidden fruit because you're afraid you'll be caught doesn't earn you moral credit. After all, you're only acting out of self-interest. If paradise suffered a power cut and the surveillance was temporarily down, you'd be in there straight away with the other looters.

"Does Surveillance Make Us Morally Better?," Emrys Westacott, Philosophy Now Magazine, June/July 2016. Emrys Westcott is professor of philosophy at Alfred University, Alfred, New York. This article first appeared in Philosophy Now, Issue 79, 2010. Reprinted by permission of the author.

So what would be the right reason for not eating the fruit? Well, God is really no different than any other parent. All he wants is absolute, unquestioning obedience (which, by an amazing coincidence, also happens to be exactly what every child wants from their parents). But God wants this obedience to be voluntary. And, very importantly, He wants it to flow from the right motive. He wants right actions to be driven not by fear, but by love for Him and reverence for what is right. (Okay, He did say to Adam, "If you eat from the tree of knowledge you will die"—which can sound a little like a threat—but grant me some literary license here.)

Moral philosophers will find themselves on familiar ground here. On this interpretation, God is a follower of the eighteenth century German philosopher Immanuel Kant. (This would, of course, come as no surprise to Kant.) According to Kant, our actions are right when they conform to the moral rules dictated to us by our reason, and they have moral worth insofar as they are motivated by respect for that moral law. In other words, my actions have moral worth if I do what is right *because I want to do the right thing*. If I don't steal someone's iPod (just another kind of Apple, really) because I think it would be wrong to do so, then I get a moral pat on the back and am entitled to polish my halo. If I don't steal the iPod because I'm afraid of getting caught, then I may be doing the right thing, and I may be applauded for being prudent, but I shouldn't be given any *moral* credit.

Highway Star

These musings are intended to frame a set of questions: What is the likely impact of ubiquitous surveillance on our moral personalities? How might the advent of the surveillance society affect a person's moral education and development? How does it alter the opportunities for moral growth? Does it render obsolete the Kantian emphasis on acting from a sense of duty as opposed to acting out of self-interest? Such questions fall under the rubric of a new field of research called Surveillance Impact Assessment.

Here is one way of thinking: surveillance edifies—that is, it builds moral character—by bringing duty and self-interest closer together. This outlook would probably be favoured by philosophers such as Plato and Thomas Hobbes. The reasoning is fairly simple: the better the surveillance, the more likely it is that moral transgressions will be detected and punished. Knowing this, people are less inclined to break the rules, and over time they form ingrained rule-abiding habits. The result is fewer instances of moral failure, and patterns of behaviour conducive to social harmony. A brief history of traffic surveillance illustrates the idea nicely:

Stage One («the state of nature»): Do whatever you please— it's a free for all. Drive as fast as you want, in whatever condition you happen to be in. Try to avoid head-on collisions. Life is fast, fun and short.

Stage Two: The government introduces speed limits, but since they are not enforced they're widely ignored.

Stage Three: Cops start patrolling the highways to enforce the speed limits. This inhibits a few would-be tearaways, but if you're clever you can still beat the rap; for instance, by knowing where the police hang out, by tailing some other speedster, or by souping up your car so the fuzz can't catch you.

Stage Four: More cops patrol the highways, and now they have radar technology. Speeding becomes decidedly imprudent, especially on holiday weekends or if you're driving past small rural villages that need to raise revenue.

At this point you can respond in one of three ways:

A) Fight fire with fire: equip your car with fuzz-busting anti-surveillance technology, and revert to your criminal ways.

B) Buy a car with cruise control and effortlessly avoid transgression;

C) Carry on as before, monitoring your speed continually and keeping an eye out at all times for likely police hiding spots. Those who choose this option are less likely than the cruise controllers to doze off, but they'll find driving more stressful.

Stage Five: To outflank the fuzz-busters, police use cameras, and eventually satellite monitors, which become increasingly hard to evade. Detection and prosecution become automated, so speeding becomes just stupid. The majority now obey the law and drive more safely.

Stage Six: Cars are equipped by law with devices that read the speed limit on any stretch of road they're on. The car's computer then acts as a governor, preventing the car from exceeding the limit. Now virtually every driver is un upstanding law-abiding citizen. If you want to speed you have to really go out of your way and tamper with the mechanism—an action analogous to what Kant would call "radical evil," which is where a person positively desires to do wrong.

It's easy to see the advantages of each successive stage in this evolution of traffic surveillance. At the end of the process, there are no more tearaways or drunk drivers endangering innocent road users. Driving is more relaxing. There are fewer accidents, less pain, less grief, less guilt, reduced demands on the health care system, lower insurance premiums, fewer days lost at work, a surging stock market, and so on. A similar story could be told with respect to drunk driving, with breathalyzers performing the same function as speed radar, and the ideal conclusion being a world in which virtually every car is fitted with a lock that shuts the engine off if the driver's blood alcohol concentration is above a certain limit. With technology taking over, surveillance becomes cheaper, and the police are freed up to catch crooked politicians and bankers running dubious schemes. Lawbreaking moves from being risky, to being foolish, to being almost inconceivable.

But there is another perspective—the one informed by Kantian ethics. On this view, increased surveillance may carry certain utilitarian benefits, but the price we pay is a diminution of our moral character. Yes, we do the wrong thing less often; in that sense, surveillance might seem to make us better. But it also stunts our growth as moral individuals.

From this point of view, moral growth involves moving closer to the saintly ideal of being someone who only ever wants to do what is right. Kant describes such an individual as having (or being) a "holy will," suggesting thereby that this condition is not attainable for ordinary human beings. For us, the obligation to be moral always feels like a burden. Wordsworth captures this well when he describes moral duty as the "stern daughter of the voice of God." Why morality feels like a burden is no mystery: there is always something we (or at least some part of us) would sooner be doing than being virtuous. We always have inclinations that conflict with what we know our duty to be. But the saintly ideal is still something we can and should aim at. Ubiquitous surveillance is like a magnetic force that changes the trajectory of our moral aspiration. We give up pursuing the holy grail of Kant's ideal, and settle for a functional but uninspiring pewter mug. Since we rarely have to choose between what's right and what's in our self-interest, our moral selves become not so much *worse* as *smaller*, withered from lack of exercise. Our moral development is arrested, and we end up on moral autopilot.

Purity vs Pragmatism?

Now I expect many people's response to this sort of anxiety about moral growth will be scathing. Here are four possible reasons for not losing sleep over it:

1) It is a merely abstract academic concern. Surely, no matter how extensive and intrusive surveillance becomes, everyday life will still yield plenty of occasions when we experience growth-promoting moral tension: for instance, in the choices we have to make over how to treat family, friends, and acquaintances.

2) The worry is perfectly *foolish*—analogous to Nietzsche's complaint that long periods of peace and prosperity shrink the soul since they offer few opportunities for battlefield heroics and sacrifice. Our ideal should be a world in which people live pleasanter lives, and where the discomfort of moral tension is largely a thing of the past. We might draw an analogy with the religious experience of sinfulness. The sense of sin may have once helped deepen human self-awareness, but that doesn't mean we should try to keep it alive today. The sense of sin has passed its sell-by date; and the same can be said of the saintly ideal.

3) The saintly ideal is and always was misguided anyway. What matters is not what people desire, but what they do. Excessive concern for people's appetites and desires is a puritan hangover. Surveillance improves behaviour, period. That is all we need to concern ourselves with.

4) Kantians should welcome surveillance, since ultimately it leads to the achievement of the very ideal they posit: the more complete the surveillance, the more duty and self-interest coincide. Surveillance technology replaces the idea of an all-seeing God who doles out just rewards and punishments, and it is more effective, since its presence, and the bad consequences of ignoring it, are much more tangibly evident. Consequently, it fosters good habits, and these habits are internalized to the point where wrongdoing becomes almost inconceivable.

That is surely just what parents and teachers aim for much of the time. As I send my kids out into the world, I don't say to myself, "I do hope they remember they have a duty not to kill, kidnap, rape, steal, torture animals or mug old ladies." I assume that for them, as for the great majority in a stable, prosperous society, such wrongdoings are inconceivable: they simply don't appear on the horizon of possible actions; and that is what I want. This inconceivability of most kinds of wrongdoing is a platform we want to be able to take for granted, and surveillance is a legitimate and effective means of building it. So, far from undermining the saintly ideal, surveillance offers a fast track to it.

Scrutiny vs Probity?

This would be a nice place to end. A trend is identified, an anxiety is articulated, but in the end the doubts are convincingly put to rest. Hobbes and Kant link arms and head off to the bar to drink a toast to their newly-discovered common ground.

But matters are not that simple. Wittgenstein warns philosophers against feeding on a diet of one-sided examples, and we need to be wary of that danger here. Indeed, I think that some other examples indicate not just that Kant may have a point, but that most of us implicitly recognize this point.

For instance, imagine you are visiting two colleges. At Scrutiny College, the guide proudly points out that each examination room is equipped with several cameras, all linked to a central monitoring station. Electronic jammers can be activated to prevent examinees from using cell phones or Blackberries. The IT department writes its own cutting-edge plagiarism-detection software. And there is zero tolerance for academic dishonesty: one strike and you're out on your ear. As a result, says the guide, there is less cheating at Scrutiny than on any other campus in the country. Students quickly see that cheating is a mug's game, and after a while no-one even considers it.

By contrast, Probity College operates on a straightforward honour system. Students sign an integrity pledge at the beginning of each academic year. At Probity, professors commonly assign take-home exams, and leave rooms full of test takers unproctored. Nor does anyone bother with plagiarism-detecting software such as *Turnitin.com*. The default assumption is that students can be trusted not to cheat.

Which college would you prefer to attend? Which would you recommend to your own kids?

Or compare two workplaces. At Scrutiny Inc., all computer activity is monitored, with regular random audits to detect and discourage any inappropriate use of company time and equipment, such as playing games, emailing friends, listening to music, or visiting internet sites that cause blood to flow rapidly from the brain to other parts of the body. At Probity Inc., on the other hand, employees are simply trusted to get their work done. Scrutiny Inc. claims to have the lowest rate of time-theft and the highest productivity of any company in its field. But where would you choose to work?

One last example. In the age of cell phones and GPS technology, it is possible for a parent to monitor their child's whereabouts at all times. They have cogent reasons for doing so. It slightly reduces certain kinds of risk to the teenager, and significantly reduces parental anxiety. It doesn't scar the youngster's psyche—after all, they were probably first placed under electronic surveillance in their crib when they were five days old! Most pertinently, it keeps them on the straight and narrow. If they go somewhere other than where they've said they'll go, or if they lie afterwards about where they've been, they'll be found out, and suffer the penalties —like, their cell phone plan will be downgraded from platinum to regular (assuming they have real hard-ass parents). But how many parents really think that this sort of surveillance of their teenage kids is a good idea?

Surveillance Suggestions

What do these examples tell us? I think they suggest a number of things.

First, the Kantian ideal still resonates with us. If we regarded the development of moral character as completely empty, misguided or irrelevant, we would be less troubled by the practices of Scrutiny College or Mom and Pop Surveillance.

Second, the fear that surveillance can actually become so extensive as to threaten an individual's healthy moral development is reasonable, for the growth of surveillance is not confined to small, minor or contained areas of our lives: it seems to be irresistibly spreading everywhere, percolating into the nooks and crannies of everyday existence, which is where much of a person's moral education occurs.

Third, our attitude to surveillance is obviously different in different settings, and this tells us something important about our hopes, fears, expectations and ideals regarding the relationship between scrutinizer and scrutinizee. The four relationships we have discussed are: state and citizen; employer and employee; teacher and student, and parent and child. In the first two cases, we don't worry much about the psychological effect of surveillance. For instance, I expect most of us would readily support improved surveillance of income in order to reduce tax evasion. But we generally assume that government, like employers, should stay out of the moral edification business.

It is possible to regard colleges in the same way. On this view, college is essentially a place where students expand their knowledge and develop certain skills. As in the workplace, surveillance levels should be determined according to what best promotes these institutional goals. However, many people see colleges as having a broader mission—as not just a place to acquire some technical training and a diploma. This broader mission includes helping students achieve personal growth, a central part of which is moral development. Edification is then seen not just as a happy side-effect of the college experience, but as one of its important and legitimate purposes. This, I think, is the deeper reason why we are perturbed by the resemblance between Scrutiny College and a prison. Our concern is not just that learning will suffer in an atmosphere of distrust: it is also that the educational mission of the college has become disappointingly narrow.

Finally, most of us agree that the moral education of children is and should be one of the goods a family secures. If not there, then where? So one good reason for parents not to install a camera over the cookie jar is that children need to experience the struggle between obligation and inclination. They even need to experience what it feels like to break the rules and get away with it; to break the rules and get caught; to break the rules, lie about it and not get caught; and so on. To reference Wordsworth again, in his autobiographical poem "The Prelude," the emergence of the young boy's moral awareness is connected to an incident when Wordsworth stole a rowing boat one evening to go for the eighteenth century equivalent of a joy ride. No-one catches him, but he becomes aware that his choices have a moral dimension.

This is not the only reason to avoid cluttering up the house with disobedience detectors, of course. Another purpose served by the family is to establish mutually-satisfying loving relationships. Moreover, the family is not simply a means to this end; the goal is internal to the practice of family life. Healthy relationships are grounded on trust, yet surveillance often signifies a lack of trust. For this reason, its effect on any relationship is corrosive. And the closer the relationship, the more objectionable we find it. Imagine how you'd feel if your spouse wanted to monitor your every coming and going.

These two objections to surveillance within the family— it inhibits moral development, and it signifies distrust—are connected, since the network of reasonably healthy relationships provided by a reasonably functional family is a primary setting for most people's moral education. The positive experience of trusting relationships, in which the default expectation is that everyone will fulfill their obligations to one another, is in itself edifying. It is surely more effective at fostering the internalization of cherished values than intimidation through surveillance. Everyone who strives to create such relationships within their family shows by their practice that they believe this to be so.

Conclusions

The upshot of these reflections is that the relation between surveillance and moral edification is complicated. In some contexts, surveillance helps keep us on track and thereby reinforces good habits that become second nature. In other contexts, it can hinder moral development by steering us away from or obscuring the saintly ideal of genuinely disinterested action. And that ideal is worth keeping alive.

Some will object that the saintly ideal is utopian. And it is. But utopian ideals are valuable. It's true that they do not help us deal with specific, concrete, short-term problems, such as how to keep drunk drivers off the road, or how to ensure that people pay their taxes. Rather, like a distant star, they provide a fixed point that we can use to navigate by. Ideals help us to take stock every so often of where we are, of where we're going, and of whether we really want to head further in that direction.

Ultimately, the ideal college is one in which every student is genuinely interested in learning and needs neither extrinsic motivators to encourage study, nor surveillance to deter cheating. Ultimately, the ideal society is one in which, if taxes are necessary, everyone pays them as freely and cheerfully as they pay their dues to some club of which they are devoted members—where citizen and state can trust each other perfectly. We know our present society is a long way from such ideals, yet we should be wary of practices that take us ever further from them. One of the goals of moral education is to cultivate a conscience—the little voice inside telling us that we should do what is right because it is right. As surveillance becomes increasingly ubiquitous, however, the chances are reduced that conscience will ever be anything more than the little voice inside telling us that someone, somewhere, may be watching.

Surveillance Cameras Are a Slippery Slope

American Civil Liberties Union of Illinois

The American Civil Liberties Union (ACLU) is a nonprofit, nonpartisan organization, dedicated to protecting freedom, liberty, equality, and justice for all within the United States.

C hicago has our nation's most "extensive and integrated" network of government video surveillance cameras, according to former U.S. Homeland Security Secretary Michael Chertoff. While the City of Chicago is secretive about the number of cameras (as well as many other critical aspects of its camera program), the City does not dispute the repeated public reports that it has access to 10,000 publicly and privately owned cameras throughout the City. In the downtown district, virtually every segment of the public way is under video surveillance. These technologically sophisticated cameras have the power to automatically identify and track particular persons, and the capacity to magnify and make visible small details and objects at great distances.

Nevertheless, the City seeks to expand and enhance the level of surveillance. Mayor Daley has announced a plan to place a camera "on every corner" of the City. In the words of another top City official, the objective is to "cover one end of the city to the other."

The American Civil Liberties Union of Illinois believes that Chicago does not need a camera on every sidewalk, on every block, in every neighborhood. Rather, our City needs to change course, before we awake to find that we cannot walk into a bookstore or a doctor's office free from the government's watchful eye.

We urge the City to order a moratorium on the expansion of the camera system. Then the City should initiate a thorough and open review of this surveillance system, including whether to reduce

Excerpt, "Chicago's Video Surveillance Cameras: A Pervasive and Unregulated Threat to Our Privacy," ACLU of Illinois, February 2011. Reprinted by permission.

the number of cameras. Finally, for those cameras that remain, the City should implement new rules to safeguard individual privacy.

The ACLU hopes that this report—the first large-scale, independent analysis of Chicago's camera system—will contribute to an informed public dialogue about the future of Chicago's system of surveillance cameras.

Chicago's Surveillance Cameras

Many of Chicago's cameras are highly visible to the general public, like the more than 1,000 cameras with flashing blue lights installed by the Chicago Police Department. Many others are unmarked or invisible. Under a program known as "Operation Virtual Shield," all of these public and private cameras are integrated together, and monitored by the City's Office of Emergency Management and Communications ("OEMC").

In addition to vast numbers and tight integration, Chicago's cameras have three powerful and potentially invasive technologies:

- The cameras have a "pan-tilt-zoom" capacity, meaning operators can increase substantially the size of the captured images.
- The cameras have a "facial recognition" capacity, meaning a computer can automatically search for a particular person's face.
- The cameras have an "automatic tracking" capacity, meaning a computer can automatically track a person or vehicle moving along the public way, jumping from one camera to the next.

All three of these technologies far exceed the powers of ordinary human observation, and dramatically increase the power of the government to watch the public.

The reach and expanse of the Chicago surveillance camera system also serves as a catalyst for other communities to expand their own systems. At least ten other Illinois communities have installed law enforcement video surveillance cameras. Although these systems are not as large, integrated, or powerful as Chicago's network, other communities clearly are following Chicago's lead.

The Problems with Chicago's Surveillance Cameras

Chicago's camera network invades the freedom to be anonymous in public places, a key aspect of the fundamental American right to be left alone. For City residents, the personal habits of daily life are carried out on our streets and sidewalks.

While earlier camera systems tracked only how some people spend some of their time in the public way, a camera on every corner—coupled with pan-tilt-zoom, facial recognition, and automatic tracking—results in government power to track how all people spend all of their time in the public way.

Each of us then will wonder whether the government is watching and recording us when we walk into a psychiatrist's office, a reproductive health care center, a political meeting, a theater performance, or a book store. While the dystopia described by George Orwell in "1984" has not yet been realized, Chicago's current 10,000 surveillance cameras are a significant step in this direction. And a camera "on every corner" would be an even greater step.

Further, Chicago's growing camera network is part of an expanding culture of surveillance in America. Combined with other government surveillance technologies (such as seizure of phone, email, and credit card records, RFID chips, and GPS devices), cameras can turn our lives into open books for government scrutiny.

Moreover, Chicago's camera network chills and deters lawful expressive activities protected by the First Amendment, like attending a political demonstration in the public way. Chicago has a long history of unlawful political surveillance, including the notorious "Red Squad" of the Chicago Police Department, which violated the rights of thousands of innocent people from the 1920s through the 1970s. Today, the Chicago police film political demonstrations, so long as the police believe they comply with the

City's nebulous requirement of a "proper law enforcement purpose." Reasonable people will respond to past and present Chicago police practices by staying away from controversial events.

Chicago officials will not say whether any of its employees have been accused of abusing the camera system. Other cities have seen abuses from much less extensive camera systems. Male camera operators have ogled women. Sensitive images have been improperly disclosed—like the image of a person committing suicide, which was later posted to a violent pornography website. A study from England found that camera operators targeted black civilians, substantially out of proportion to both their suspicious conduct and their presence in the population being monitored.

Finally, it is important to consider what Chicagoans are not getting, because of the more than $60 million that the City has spent on our nation's largest and most integrated camera network. For example, these taxpayer funds might have helped fill the 1,000 vacancies in Chicago's understaffed police force.

In light of these civil liberties and civil rights concerns, the ACLU opposes the unreviewed expansion of Chicago's camera system, and the absence of critical privacy regulations, even if the camera system were proven to reduce crime. In any event, numerous studies by independent scholars have concluded that video surveillance cameras in fact do not reduce violent crime, and only in certain circumstances reduce property crime (such as in parking garages). While the City asserts that its cameras reduce crime, it has not supported this assertion with methodologically sound reports or underlying statistical data. Also, while the City asserts that its cameras have led to 4,500 arrests in the last 4 years, that is less than 1% of all the arrests during that time.

The ACLU's Proposals

Given the many grave problems created by Chicago's cameras, and the lack of proof that they are effective, the ACLU of Illinois offers the following proposals.

First, there should be a moratorium on the deployment of more cameras.

Second, during this moratorium, there should be a comprehensive review of the past, present, and future of Chicago's surveillance camera system. This review should define the City's objectives, consider all of the costs, and weigh all of the evidence about effectiveness. This review should be conducted in the open, and solicit the input of the general public. Perhaps most importantly, this review should consider whether to reduce the number of cameras in the City's system.

Third, for the cameras that remain operational, there should be new safeguards to protect the privacy and other rights of the public. Specifically, the City should:

1. Pan-Tilt-Zoom ("PTZ")

a) Require individualized reasonable suspicion either of criminal activity or of a threat to public safety, before a camera operator uses the PTZ function to magnify the image of a particular person, or anything in his possession.

b) Require individualized reasonable suspicion either of criminal activity or of a threat to public safety, before a camera operator uses the PTZ function to either aim a camera at activity protected by the First Amendment, or to magnify such activity.

c) Prohibit camera operators from considering race, national origin, ethnicity, religion, gender, sexual orientation, or sexual identity when deciding whether to use the PTZ function to aim a camera at a particular person, or to magnify the image of a particular person—except when there is a "look-out" order providing specific information linking a person with one of these demographic characteristics to a particular criminal incident.

2. Facial Recognition and Automatic Tracking

Require probable cause either of criminal activity or of a threat to public safety, before using the camera system to perform facial recognition or automatic tracking of a particular individual.

3. Recording Private Areas

Prohibit the use of cameras to record activities taking place in private areas, such as a private residence or business. (While a CPD training DVD states this rule, it does not currently appear in a written policy.)

4. Retention of Camera Images

Prohibit retention of cameras images (beyond a short period of time, such as 7 days), unless a supervisor determines that (1) there is reasonable suspicion that the images in question contain evidence of criminal activity, or (2) the images are relevant to an ongoing investigation or pending criminal trial.

5. Dissemination of Camera Images

Prohibit dissemination of camera images to third parties, except that a supervisor can disseminate images:

a) To another governmental agency, if (1) there is reasonable suspicion that the images in question contain evidence of criminal activity, or (2) the images are relevant to an ongoing investigation or pending criminal trial.

b) To a criminal defendant, if the images in question are related to the pending charges.

6. Periodic Audits

Require:

a) An annual audit of the City's camera systems to identify and evaluate:

(1) the effectiveness of the cameras at reducing crime or achieving some other legitimate government purpose;

(2) the impact of the cameras on the privacy and other civil rights and civil liberties of the general public; and

(3) any misuse of the cameras, and the corrective action taken.

b)   Public disclosure of such audits, including all electronic statistical data used to evaluate camera effectiveness.

7. Public Notice

Require:

a)   Public notice and an opportunity to be heard prior to installation of any new cameras.

b)   Public notice of the location of all cameras linked to the City's camera network.

8. Enforcement

Require:

a)   Supervisory review of camera operators to ensure their compliance with the rules herein, and any other rules regarding the City's cameras that protect the privacy and other civil rights and civil liberties of the general public.

b)   Investigation of all camera operators alleged to have violated such rules.

c)   Discipline of all camera operators found to have violated such rules.

9. Linked Private Cameras

As to all private sector cameras that are linked into the City's camera network, apply all of the rules herein, and any other rules regarding the City's cameras that protect the privacy and other civil rights and civil liberties of the general public.

10. Traffic Enforcement Cameras

a) Pictures may be taken only while a traffic infraction is occurring.

b) Pictures may be taken only of the vehicle and license plate, and not of the face of the motorist or passengers.

c) Pictures may be used only for the enforcement of a traffic infraction.

d) Pictures shall be destroyed upon completion of the enforcement of a traffic infraction.

e) Intersections with traffic enforcement cameras shall be clearly marked.

The ACLU's Investigation

The ACLU of Illinois has investigated the nature, scope, capacity, and regulation of Chicago's system of video surveillance cameras. The ACLU has reviewed the information in the public domain, including government records and media accounts. Moreover, the ACLU used the Illinois Freedom of Information Act ("FOIA") to obtain records from the City, including policies, forms, a training DVD, reports regarding effectiveness, and contracts providing City access to private cameras. The law firm of Miller Shakman & Beem served as ACLU co-counsel in the administrative enforcement of this FOIA request. Unfortunately, the City refused to state whether it has additional policy and training records; refused to disclose any records concerning alleged misuse of the cameras, or even to state whether there have been such allegations; and did not disclose any electronic data, including the data underlying the effectiveness reports. The ACLU also used FOIA to obtain records from many other Illinois communities that use video surveillance cameras.

In March 2010, the ACLU repeatedly asked the City for permission to visit the Operations Center of the OEMC, in order to view and better understand the nerve center of the City's camera system. Unfortunately, the City did not respond.

In April 2010, the ACLU sent the City a letter proposing the new regulations stated above. Again, the City did not respond.

This lack of transparency and unresponsiveness concerning a partially covert surveillance system bodes ill for the residents of Chicago, of whom 10,000 are ACLU members and supporters.

Organizations to Contact

The editors have compiled the following list of organizations concerned with the issues debated in this book. The descriptions are derived from materials provided by the organizations. All have publications or information available for interested readers. This list was compiled on the date of publication of the present volume; the information provided here may change. Be aware that many organizations take several weeks or longer to respond to inquiries, so allow as much time as possible.

American Civil Liberties Union (ACLU)
125 Broad Street, 18th Floor, New York, NY 10004
(212) 549-2500
website: www.aclu.org

For nearly 100 years, the ACLU has been our nation's guardian of liberty, working in courts, legislatures, and communities to defend and preserve the individual rights and liberties that the Constitution and the laws of the United States guarantee everyone in this country. With more than a million members, activists, and supporters, the ACLU is a nationwide organization that fights tirelessly in all fifty states, Puerto Rico, and Washington, DC, to safeguard everyone's rights.

Consumer Watchdog
(310) 392-0522
website: www.consumerwatchdog.org

Consumer Watchdog is a nonprofit organization dedicated to providing an effective voice for taxpayers and consumers in an era when special interests dominate public discourse, government, and politics. Consumer Watchdog deploys an in-house team of public interest lawyers, policy experts, strategists, and grassroots activists to expose, confront, and change corporate and political injustice every day, saving Americans billions of dollars and improving countless lives.

Electronic Frontier Foundation (EEF)

815 Eddy Street, San Francisco, CA 94109
(415) 436 9333
email: info@eff.org
website: www.eff.org

The Electronic Frontier Foundation is the leading nonprofit organization defending civil liberties in the digital world. EFF champions user privacy, free expression, and innovation through impact litigation, policy analysis, grassroots activism, and technology development. We work to ensure that rights and freedoms are enhanced and protected as our use of technology grows.

Electronic Privacy Information Center (EPIC)

Electronic Privacy Information Center, 1718 Connecticut Avenue NW, Suite 200, Washington, DC 20009
email: info@epic.org
website: www.epic.org

EPIC is a public interest research center established to focus public attention on emerging privacy issues and to protect privacy, freedom of expression, and democratic values in the information age. EPIC pursues a wide range of program activities including policy research, public education, conferences, litigation, publications, and advocacy. EPIC routinely files amicus briefs in federal courts, pursues open government cases, defends consumer privacy, organizes conferences for NGOs, and speaks before Congress and judicial organizations about emerging privacy and civil liberties issues.

National Security Agency (NSA)
9800 Savage Road, Suite 6272,
Fort George G. Meade, MD 20755-6000
(301) 688-6524
website: www.nsa.gov

The National Security Agency/Central Security Service (NSA/CSS) leads the US government in cryptology that encompasses both signals intelligence (SIGINT) and information assurance (IA) products and services, and enables computer network operations (CNO) in order to gain a decision advantage for the United States and its allies under all circumstances.

Office of the Director of National Intelligence
Office of the Director of National Intelligence, Washington, DC 20511
(703) 733-8600
website: https://www.dni.gov

Created after the terror attacks on September 11, 2011, the Office of the Director of National Intelligence leads intelligence integration and forges an intelligence community that delivers the most insightful information in order to ensure the security of the nation.

The Privacy Coalition
Electronic Privacy Information Center, 1718 Connecticut Avenue NW, Suite 200, Washington, DC 20009
email: coalition@privacy.org
website: https://privacycoalition.org

The Privacy Coalition is a nonpartisan coalition of consumer, civil liberties, educational, family, library, labor, and technology organizations that have agreed to the Privacy Pledge, a promise to support a privacy framework to safeguard the rights of Americans in this information age.

Privacy International

62 Britton Street, London, EC1M 5UY, United Kingdom
+44 (0) 20 3422 4321
email: info@privacyinternational.org
website: www.privacyinternational.org

Privacy International is committed to fighting for the right to privacy across the world. The organization investigates the secret world of government surveillance and exposes the companies enabling it. They litigate to ensure that surveillance is consistent with the rule of law and advocate for strong national, regional, and international laws that protect privacy.

Wikileaks

website: https://wikileaks.org

WikiLeaks is a multinational media organization and associated library. WikiLeaks specializes in the analysis and publication of large datasets of censored or otherwise restricted official materials involving war, spying, and corruption. It has so far published more than ten million documents and associated analyses.

The World Wide Web Consortium (W3C)
Technology and Society Domain Privacy Interest Group

website: www.w3.org

The World Wide Web Consortium (W3C) is an international community where member organizations, a full-time staff, and the public work together to develop Web standards. Led by web inventor Tim Berners-Lee and CEO Jeffrey Jaffe, W3C's mission is to lead the web to its full potential.

Bibliography

Julia Angwin. *Dragnet Nation: A Quest for Privacy, Security, and Freedom in a World of Relentless Surveillance.* New York, NY: Henry Holt and Company, 2014.

David Barnard-Wills. *Surveillance and Identity: Discourse, Subjectivity and the State.* Burlington, VT: Ashgate, 2011.

Anthony C. Caputo. *Digital Video Surveillance and Security.* Amsterdam, NL: Butterworth-Heinemann, 2014.

Roy Coleman and Michael McCahill. *Surveillance & Crime.* Los Angeles, CA: 2011.

William Eyre. *The Real ID Act: Privacy and Government Surveillance.* El Paso, TX: LFB Scholarly Publishing, 2011.

BJ Goold. *Surveillance.* New York, NY: Routledge, 2009.

Glenn Greenwald. *No Place to Hide: Edward Snowden, the NSA, and the U.S. Surveillance State.* New York, NY: Metopolitan Books/Henry Holt, 2014.

Joseph G. Massingale. *Digital Surveillance: Laws, Security, and Related Issues.* New York, NY: Nova Science Publishers, 2009.

Torin Monahan. *Surveillance in the Time of Insecurity.* New Brunswick, NJ: Rutgers University Press, 2010.

Adam D. Moore. *Privacy, Security and Accountability: Ethics, Law and Policy.* Lanham, MD: Rowman & Littlefield International, 2015.

Robert Plotkin *Privacy, Security, and Cyberspace.* New York, NY: Facts On File, 2012.

Lauri S. Scherer. *Privacy.* Detroit, MI: Greenhaven Press, 2014.

Sophie Stalla-Bourdillon, Joshua Phillips, and Mark Ryan. *Privacy vs. Security.* London, UK: Springer, 2014.

Eric Stoddart. *Theological Perspectives on a Surveillance Society: Watching and Being Watched.* Burlington, VT: Ashgate, 2011.

Daniel Trottier. *Social Media As Surveillance: Rethinking Visibility in a Converging World.* Burlington, VT: Ashgate, 2012.

Brett J. Wills. *The Foreign Intelligence Surveillance Act and its Ramifications.* New York, NY: 2010.

Index